R.S. Thomas

SELECTED PROSE

R.S.Thomas, May 1983

R.S. Thomas

SELECTED PROSE

edited by Sandra Anstey
with an Introduction by Ned Thomas

POETRY WALES PRESS
1983

PUBLISHED BY POETRY WALES PRESS
56 PARCAU AVENUE, BRIDGEND, MID GLAMORGAN

British Library Cataloguing in Publication Data

Thomas, R. S.
  Selected Prose.
  I. Title   II. Anstey, Sandra
  828/.914   PR6039.H618

ISBN 0-907476-27-9

The publisher acknowledges the financial assistance of the Welsh Arts Council.

Cover and frontispiece photographs: Welsh Arts Coucil.
Cover design: Cloud Nine Design.
Drawings in 'Dau Gapel' by permission of Mildred Eldridge.

PRINTED IN 11pt BASKERVILLE II
BY
D. BROWN & SONS LIMITED
BRIDGEND, MID GLAMORGAN

Contents

Acknowledgements

The editor would like to thank the following for permission to reprint copyright material:

Penguin Books Ltd., for the 'Introduction to *The Penguin Book of Religious Verse*'; the University of Wales Press for *Words and the Poet*; the Welsh Library Association for 'The Making of a Poem'; Faber & Faber Publishers for the 'Introduction to *A Choice of Wordsworth's Verse*'; Gwasg Gomer for 'The Paths Gone By', first published in *Y Llwybrau Gynt 2*; 'The Abercuawg Lecture' is translated from the original Welsh published by Gwasg Gomer on behalf of the National Eisteddfod Court.

Thanks are also due to Brynley F. Roberts, Rhiannon H. Brown and her colleagues in the Library of the University College of Swansea, Mick Felton and Cary Archard of Poetry Wales Press, and of course to R. S. Thomas.

Editor's Note

In this, the first selection of R. S. Thomas's prose, I have chosen pieces that illustrate the writer's breadth of interest and development of concerns through the years. An indication of the range of material available is given in the bibliography that I have compiled for the closing pages of this book.

Six of the pieces chosen appeared originally in Welsh, and each of the translations from the Welsh here included has its own complicated history. Suffice it to say that the great bulk of the work on *Abercuawg*, *Y Llwybrau Gynt* and the review of *Bury My Heart at Wounded Knee* was done by John Phillips as part of a project in the Department of English at the UCW Aberystwyth, though Tony Bianchi and Catherine Thomas also had a hand in the work. 'Dau Gapel' was translated by Catherine Thomas, and 'Hunanladdiad Y Llenor' by Gwyn Davies. Ned Thomas translated 'Llenyddiaeth Eingl-Gymreig' and he also undertook the final revision of each translation before publication. R. S. Thomas's willingness to answer numerous queries was appreciated throughout.

I have added footnotes to most of the extracts that appear in this selection, providing source references and translations that may be of interest to the reader.

Sandra Anstey

Introduction

Each reader will find his or her own particular focus of interest and special pleasures in this selection from R.S.Thomas's prose. First, there are the pleasures of recognition—a phrase or an image in a poem can be traced to an experience recorded in prose, and this then allows us to measure what the poem has made of that experience. Thus it is with that marvellous description in his autobiographical radio talk of the autumn in Manafon:

> And then after a long, hot summer, the leaves would start to change colour, and for two months the valley would be like a fairyland: the cherry-trees dark red and the ash-trees yellow. There was a large ash-tree at the end of the Rectory lane which would be completely yellow by November. The leaves remained on it one autumn longer than usual. But there was heavy frost one night and the next day as the sun rose, the leaves began to fall. They went on falling for hours making the tree like a golden fountain playing silently in the sun; I shall never forget it.

This tree reappears in 'The Bush' (*Later Poems*, 1983):

> And in this country
> of failure, the rain
> falling out of a black
> cloud in gold pieces there
> are none to gather,
> I have thought often
> of the fountain of my people
> that played beautifully here
> once in the sun's light
> like a tree undressing.

There are many such comparisons to be made, and one is tempted to quote them all.

But although never irrelevant to his poetry, R.S.Thomas's prose pieces also have an interest in their own right. They claim attention as the product of a mind that, standing so far aside from the fashions of its day as to have seemed sometimes badly out of touch, now often surprises us with its challenging modernity. His review of *Bury My Heart at Wounded Knee* is a case in point.

The questions which R.S.Thomas raises and the themes to which he returns have been ably and amply surveyed by Randal Jenkins,[1] which allows this introduction to take another direction. I believe that the prose is of immense help towards understanding the overall shape of the poet's work, and I shall give my interpretation of what that shape is.

The unity of a writer's work is never entirely easy to see from close by, and Anthony Conran has suggested in *The Cost of Strangeness* (1982) that there is a special precariousness to the unity of the work of Anglo-Welsh writers deriving from the lack of a tradition and very often from personal uncertainties or variations in what they think they are doing. If R.S.Thomas escapes this stricture more than most it is because he has sought to define his own position with a self-consciousness that is uncharacteristic of the Anglo-Welsh and a remorselessness towards himself that sometimes verges on masochism. Even so there are within his poetry shifts of perspective and subject-matter that are not always easy to explain in terms of the poetry itself. Add to this the existence of disparate "English" and "Welsh" critical perspectives, each drawing on different aspects of his work, and the need for a unifying frame becomes evident. The prose helps to provide that frame.

It is particularly useful that the reader of this volume has available side by side items written by R.S.Thomas in English and other items originally in Welsh. It is not so much the difference of language in itself that lends a subtle difference to the respective pieces, but the different sense of audience that goes with the use of each language. In English he often has the tone of a specialist. Sometimes he is the "priest-poet", the publishers' natural choice for an introduction to *The Penguin Book of Religious Verse* or to a selection of George Herbert's poems; sometimes he is the craftsman with excellent things to say about the effect of certain adjectives in certain places in the line. Like a Roman poet of the late empire this priest of a disestablished church in an out-of-the-way province has a mastery of the pure classical language that can scarcely be matched, but his audience is a specialised segment of the far-flung educated sector of English readers. In the Welsh pieces on the other hand, it is the whole man who speaks, and with a clear sense of speaking to his own

people. Apropos of this question of audience, it is interesting to find
R.S.Thomas saying in a short early review that all negative criticism
of Wales should be in the mother-tongue (i.e. Welsh). It is also
interesting to place side by side what he has to say about the word
"Abercuawg" in the Welsh lecture of that name, and about the
word "Jaberwocky" in the English lecture *Words and the Poet*. The
linguistic and philosophical points made about words which
correspond to nothing that exists in the "real" world are much the
same, but whereas in the one case the point made is literary and
academic, in the other it is social and political as well, and the author
can count on his *angst* over Abercuawg being shared by his listeners.

The growth of the poet's mind is nicely paralleled by the westward
spatial trajectory of his career—from the lowlands of north-east
Wales where it borders England, to Manafon in upland
Montgomeryshire, then to Eglwysfach in Ceredigion and to
Aberdaron in the Llŷn peninsula, from mainly English-speaking to
mainly Welsh-speaking areas. Looking west from the English
Marches, he tells us in his radio talk, "the sky would be aflame,
reminding one of ancient battles." There is a touch here of that late
English Romanticism found in Housman's:

> The vanquish'd eve as night prevails
> Bleeds upon the road to Wales

just as there is of Arnold's "Celtic magic" when R.S.Thomas adds
"there was in the West a land of romance and danger, a secret
land". But this kind of Romanticism comes to be rejected in the
light of the everyday experience of living among the hill-farmers of
Manafon, just as Arnold's version of the Welsh literary tradition is
rejected for Sir Idris Bell's with its emphasis on clarity and
disciplined expression.

But one cannot leave the question of Romanticism at that. One
has to speak rather of a clash of Romanticisms that is not easily
understood within the tradition of the English literature of England.
The late Romanticism of the far horizon that was so often projected
onto the Celtic West is rejected but in its place there appears a new
and fresh Romanticism, grounded in *this* place and welling up in the
heart in the manner of the great early Romantics, "central peace
subsisting at the heart of endless agitation" in Wordsworth's phrase
so often quoted by R.S.Thomas. Do those words not well describe
that sense we get in many of the poems of the uplands that amid all

the questionings, amid all the commotion of conflicting responses
which the poet discovers in himself, R.S.Thomas has found his
subject, the source of his imaginative life; the eye is quietly
concentrated:

> He was in the fields when I went out.
> He was in the fields when I came back.
> ('Truth')

or again

> With your pigs and your sheep and your sons
>   and holly-cheeked daughters
> You will continue to unwind your days
> In a crude tapestry under the jealous heavens
> To affront, bewilder, yet compel my gaze.
> ('A Priest to his People')

   Though this is not the place to do more than adumbrate a whole
theory of cultural interaction, I believe that this transplanted early
Romanticism is a social and cultural phenomenon related to the
growth of national feeling, and not only in Wales. In the West
Indian poet Derek Walcott one finds the same rejection of the
Romantic tourist's exotic or pastoral view and the same birth of a
new centre of consciousness through a sense of fusion with place and
deep communion with people. One has to say "communion" rather
than "communication" because R.S.Thomas's hill-farmers and
Walcott's fishermen do not understand the artistic perspective into
which they have walked, but they are dignified by it in the
consciousness of the reader:

> I have taxed your ignorance of rhyme and sonnet,
> Your want of deference to the painter's skill,
> But I know, as I listen, that your speech has in it
> The source of all poetry, clear as a rill
> Bubbling from your lips; and what brushwork could equal
> The artistry of your dwelling on the bare hill?
> ('A Priest to his People')

and in Walcott's poem 'Roots':

> From all that sorrow, beauty is our gain,
> Though it may not seem so
> To an old fisherman rowing home in the rain.
> (from *In a Green Night*)

For the reader the overall effect is of enlargement. There is a potent source of life and there is a mind that can perhaps one day make that life conscious of itself. When attached to a particular place and people this feeling of enlargement is a great motor of national feeling.

In several places R.S.Thomas acknowledges a Coleridgean and therefore Kantian debt, though not an unmodified allegiance. Though there are sometimes difficulties (which have been acutely formulated by Anthony Conran) in reconciling R.S.Thomas's poetry with Romantic doctrine, I believe that it does nevertheless represent his central position, and that to recognise this helps us understand a great deal. In the previous paragraph I spoke of life becoming conscious of itself. One could rephrase this as mind becoming conscious of its own life, and therefore of thought withdrawing outside the space of representation, or at most using representation as self-conscious metaphor for its own processes. One recalls the many one-sided dialogues with Prytherch which end up in 'Servant' with the solipsistic recognition: "You served me well, Prytherch", and those other dialogues across inner space with God:

> There are questions we are the solution
> to, others whose echoes we must expand
> to contain
> ('Emerging')

But it is the great Romantic images of trees and root and fountain that most satisfyingly connect R.S.Thomas with this tradition. They allow a multiplicity of comparisons, with Yeats, with the early Romantics in England and Germany, but perhaps most interestingly with the Welsh-language poet of his own generation, Waldo Williams, who also subscribed to the Coleridgean theory of the imagination and with similar unorthodox theological consequences. Such comparisons are suggested by the following extracts from R.S.Thomas's prose and poetry:

> I will simply say that I realised there was no such thing as time, but that everything is a fountain welling up endlessly from immortal God.
> ('Two Chapels')

> Summer is here.
> Once more the house has its
> Spray of martins, Proust's fountain

> Of small birds, whose light shadows
> Come and go in the sunshine
> Of the lawn as thoughts do
> In my mind.
>
>   ('The Place')

> ...A chill in the flesh
> tells him that death is not far off
> now: it is the shadow under the great boughs
> of life
>
>   ('Good')

And it will not be a forest of poles and pylons, but a leafy wood.

                                         (*Abercuawg* lecture)

> Baudelaire's grave
> not too far
> from the tree of science.
> Mine, too,
> since I sought and failed
> to steal from it,
> somewhere within sight
> of the tree of poetry
> that is eternity wearing
> the green leaves of time.
>
>   ('Prayer')

I find it interesting that the three verse extracts here are all from poems placed in the final position in their respective volumes. On the first page of this introduction I quoted two passages in which the tree and fountain images are combined as they are in one of the most discussed passages of Waldo Williams's 'Mewn Dau Gae':

> Yr oedd rhyw ffynhonnau'n torri tua'r nefoedd
> Ac yn syrthio'n ôl a'u dagrau fel dail pren.

> (The fountains burst up towards heaven, till,
> Falling back, their tears were like leaves of a tree.)
>   (tr. Anthony Conran)

It is to this celebrated image of Waldo Williams's that R.S.Thomas most probably refers in his poem 'Blondes' when, after invoking the bland simplicities of suburban domestic life he concludes:

>   the tear-laden tree
> Of a poet strikes no root in their hearts.

The doubt he here expresses shows how partial the comparison with Waldo Williams, and how selective of affirmative passages my small batch of quotations. If R.S.Thomas believes in the one great root under the branches of life, he does so in full consciousness of the spreading concrete. It often appears that Wales in his definition is that shrinking area where nature is not wholly tamed, ''the high pastures of the heart'', where the poet's tree still strikes roots, where the life of the imagination is still possible:

> But the hill remains, keeping its perennial freshness. Life with its money and its honours, its pride and its power, seems of little worth if we are to lose this. This it is that haunts men, that epitomises Wales in a phrase—the bright hill under the black cloud.
>
> (*The Mountains*)

Some of us may feel uncomfortable that this powerful image yet manages to exclude so much of the social and historical—yes, and human—reality of Wales, yet perhaps we should not consider it in representational terms at all. In *Abercuawg* the good place is not rural Wales or even a future Welsh-speaking Wales, but somewhere in a continuous process of becoming, constantly produced in a struggle that amounts to perpetual revolution.

The pressures of the modern world which turn R.S.Thomas's Wales into something with a status close to that of pure idea also have an internalized dimension in language itself. In 1946, surveying 'Some Contemporary Scottish Writing' R.S.Thomas thought he discovered signs

> that the mantle of writers like T. Gwynn Jones and W.J.Gruffydd is falling not upon the younger Welsh writers, but upon those who express themselves in English.... Ireland has contrived to remain Irish despite her use of English, and there is no overwhelming reason why we should not succeed also.... But if we choose English as that medium, have we the singleness of mind, the strength of will to remain primarily Welshmen?

R.S.Thomas's practice has shown those strengths to be amply possessed by one writer at least, but his own theoretic position had changed as early as 1952, as illustrated in an extract from 'Anglo-Welsh Literature':

> My view is this: since there is in Wales a mother-tongue that continues to flourish, a proper Welshman can only look at English as a means of rekindling interest in the Welsh-language culture, and of leading people back to the mother-tongue.

This change of attitude, which leads directly to 'The Creative Writer's Suicide' was really inevitable given the conceptual framework of Romantic theory. Language, which in eighteenth-century discussion was usually treated as simply representational, came to be thought of as living, organic, related to peoples. Herder wished to visit Scotland so as to meet "the living language of a living people." Even in the 1946 essay on Scottish writing, R.S.Thomas had quoted J.R.Lowell's requirement "the tongue of the people in the mouth of the scholar" which he found fulfilled in the work of MacDiarmid's younger compatriots; but he did not pursue the implications for Welsh writers using English, who had no equivalent of Scots, literary or spoken. His remarks here and there on the English dialect of Montgomeryshire, and poems such as 'The Mixen' show him exploring the possibilities of a distinct kind of English, but it is hardly the language of the Welsh people any more than "Valleys English" can be, within R.S.Thomas's definition of Wales.

The view that one was writing poetry in English so as to render that poetry unnecessary in the Wales of the future was expressed by several English-writing nationalist poets of the 'seventies, but rarely was it underwritten by such anguish and self-disgust as we find in R.S.Thomas at his bitterest:

> I was
> born into the squalor of
> their feeding and sucked their speech
> in with my mother's
> infected milk, so that whatever
> I throw up now is still theirs.
> ('It hurts him to think')

By the early 'seventies, by the time of *What is a Welshman?* from which this quotation is taken, and *H'm* (1972), one finds something very close to despair in R.S.Thomas's work. The last poem in *H'm* sees mankind as an idiot whirled about by a fairground machine. In the same volume the tree imagery has come to this:

> Among the forests
> Of metal the one human
> Sound was the lament of
> The poets for deciduous language.
> ('Postscript')

while 'Petition' closes, as Anthony Conran has observed, with lines
which scarcely support the sentiments about the "imaginative vision
of poetry" expressed by the poet in John Ormond's television
programme of 1972:

> One thing I have asked
> Of the disposer of the issues
> Of life: that truth should defer
> To beauty. It was not granted.

But these were not the last words. Subsequent volumes reaffirm if
not faith, then at least quest, and the tree imagery reasserts itself.
The Welsh dilemmas virtually disappear as subject-matter. One
cannot, of course, know all the deep changes at work in a writer, but
there is evidence in his own words for thinking that R.S.Thomas
found release from some of the intolerable tensions reflected in the
work of the early 'seventies in action outside the writing of poetry.
From the mid-seventies on he became a public figure in Wales
making numerous interventions in Welsh language campaigns and
more recently on behalf of the Campaign for Nuclear Disarmament.
He has always spoken of "the necessity for politics" and in 'The
Creative Writer's Suicide' when he has stated the impossible
dilemma of the Anglo-Welsh writer, he turns on his literary self:

> But all this is really a case of huffing and puffing while standing still!
> In the Wales in which we live, there is no literary answer to the
> literary problem.

This is the other, down-to-earth side of R.S.Thomas, who at the end
of *Abercuawg* after calling for leafy woods instead of pylons adds that
the pylons will be placed tastefully out of sight "remembering that it
is man's spirit, and not profit, which comes first", a reformist of
kinds after all! Nor is R.S.Thomas the first Welsh poet in our time to
feel the need to act outside his poetry. Waldo Williams only felt able
to write his 'Mewn Dau Gae' when he had acted in its spirit by
withholding his taxes in protest at the Korean war.

In an interview with Dylan Iorwerth broadcast on Radio Cymru
on 15 May 1983 R.S.Thomas stated that he deliberately changed his
subject-matter when he moved to Aberdaron. He felt he had had
enough of Iago Prytherch and of writing about the countryside, and
he also agreed that he no longer wrote poems which addressed
themselves directly to the problems of his country. He was then
asked:

Does this perhaps mean that previously you had been using poetry as a way of being a Welshman, of emphasising that you were a Welshman?

That was the aim of the Anglo-Welsh movement. When I started writing, Anglo-Welsh literature had come into existence, and I think every writer belonging to that school felt a certain necessity to tell the world "I am a Welshman"....

By the time I reached Llŷn I felt I had come home, I had achieved my aim—I changed my subject-matter but became more of a Welshman, a straightforward Welshman, speaking Welsh every day, and therefore I was ready to act like a Welshman, so there was no need for me to write like a Welshman.

Ned Thomas

Note
1.   'R.S.Thomas, Occasional Prose', *Poetry Wales*, VII:4 (1972), pp. 93-108.

The Depopulation of the Welsh Hill Country

Wales, V:7 (1945), pp. 75-80

The Depopulation of the Welsh Hill Country

Much has been heard about the depopulation of the Scottish Highlands and the gradual disintegration of the crofting community, and a certain measure of sympathy has been aroused, leading to strenuous if not successful efforts on the part of Scottish Nationalists to arrest the decline and rehabilitate some of the families.

It is not my intention to minimize the importance of the Scottish question, but rather to draw attention to, or enlist sympathy with a similar, if less spectacular need in my own country of Wales. Such a large proportion of the population is centred in the south, and so familiar is the problem of unemployment in the industrial areas, that the increasing depopulation of the uplands of the interior tends to pass unnoticed by all save a few keen-eyed observers. The area which comes most readily to mind, being the part with which I am best acquainted, is the hilly district of central Montgomeryshire, but I believe that it will serve as the prototype for the greater part of the Welsh uplands. It is a romantic stretch of country, containing views as striking in their way as anything in the British Isles. It is a kind of plateau, maintaining a fairly uniform level at about fourteen hundred feet, but divided here and there by small, rambling river valleys such as those of the Rhiw, the Banwy and the Twymyn. It contains an abundance of peat, and is covered by great expanses of bracken, reed and coarse, upland grass, interspersed with sudden patches of green pasture, that gleam like oases in that sand-coloured desert. In the early spring it re-echoes to the cry of innumerable curlews, which come in from the sea to breed, and about June the more marshy areas are white with the fairy-like cotton grass. It is sheep country for the most part, but increasing numbers of Hereford bullocks have been fattened there since the beginning of the war, and in the lower or more sheltered parts are to be found moderately successful small farms of a general character. The road system is poor, and there are many outlying farms or crofts with nothing more than a grass track, generally waterlogged in winter, between them and the nearest road, which is often two or three miles away.

It is, as I have said, a romantic-looking country at first sight, and a thrill of excitement runs through one, as one catches a glimpse of some grey stone building with its guardian pines, lying away out in a depression of the moor, or set boldly in the bare hillside. Who lives there? There are cattle grazing the grass below it and some sheep above. The imagination busies itself with the idea of some poetically-minded hill farmer in love with solitude, with a kitchen that might prove the perfect setting for a *noson lawen*. But wait a moment. Turn your binoculars on it and what do you find? A broken chimney and gaping windows. The place is uninhabited and is being used as a kind of dilapidated hafod, or Scotch shieling, by a neighbouring farmer, who lives somewhat nearer civilisation, but who is himself probably a mere bailiff for someone in the richer more fertile lowlands. And this holds good for scores of these old upland dwellings. In a short ramble only the other day, I passed five such, all empty, all steadily sinking back into the moorland from which they arose, for the farmers who are using them as stables or barns care nothing for their condition, since they do not belong to them, and even if they do, they have not the necessary money to keep them in repair. But even more important than the buildings which are decaying are the men who have left them, been forced to leave them, thus losing for ever their real meaning in life. The buildings remain and give a certain character to the country, but the people have gone, the people who made the district significant, who were a manifestation, and an interesting one too, of the strange spirit of life that bloweth where it listeth. Old buildings have a certain sadness of their own, it is true, but it more often derives from the life which once they sheltered within their walls, and in looking upon these piles of lichen-covered stones with their wind-twisted sentinel trees, one cannot but mourn the old life which has ceased to keep company with them, ceased to draw its nourishment from them.

A tour of any of these uplands is sufficient to prove to an acute observer just how many dwellings have fallen into desuetude, but to appreciate to the full the seriousness and the reality of the loss which these districts have sustained, let one go up alone into them, and wander there a whole day until the sun goes down and the snipe begins to drum over the dark bog, and gradually the spell of the country begins to weave itself about one, and the full realization of what has happened breaks upon one. Alongside the complete stillness and solitude there is the hush which suggests that it was but a moment ago that life fled, or rather stole away from these solid stone buildings. One approaches them softly, half expecting to find someone still clinging doggedly to his dwindling patrimony. But in most cases they have been empty for some years, the old rooms are thick with dung, and walls that appeared from a distance to be in such good repair, are now seen to be crumbling before the long siege of rain and the fretting of the wind.

So far it may appear to the reader that I am merely indulging a personal nostalgia, merely sighing a lament over something which has gone beyond recall. But I would not trespass upon the editor's valuable space merely for the sake of threnodising. The fact is that despite the many ruined homesteads in these upland districts, there are others still managing to hold out, and it is for their sake that I write.

Dotted here and there about these lovely moors, in a small defile beside a hurrying stream, or crouching for shelter beneath a few pines or firs, there are still a considerable number of small farms and crofts, whose occupants manage to win some kind of living from the grudging soil. These are the true Welsh peasantry and to know them is to feel a real affection for them. Augustus John said somewhere that a real gipsy was always worth five shillings, and so with these people, one would willingly empty one's pockets for them in return for their ready smiles and carefree ways. With a few sheep and pigs and poultry, a cow or two, and maybe a horse or a pony, they manage not only to exist, but what is incomprehensible to our modern world, they are happy too, and have no wish to change. Happy as cuckoos the lowlanders call them with something of contempt, although one suspects a certain envy there too. But, I repeat, the important thing is that they do not wish to leave. Whatever one may think of the hill subsidy it has at least in many cases been responsible for these people's being able to carry on in their native district. But there is the feeling that it has merely arrested the decline and not abolished it. And even with regard to this subsidy there are many who were in great need of it who have failed to qualify for it owing to some quibbling condition, or owing to the fact that much of the upland pasture is being grazed by stock belonging to lowlanders. Before it is too late, therefore, these people must be helped.

Oh, I know that they are not a hundred per cent. efficient, as the contemporary world of scientific planning would have it, but they more than atone for this by their character and the native colouring of their lives. Besides, they understand the land and the climate. How often has it been said that the health and wealth of a country depends upon its possession of a sturdy, flourishing peasantry? But this has become anathema to a generation that thinks only in terms of prices and statistics. Health and wealth have but one connotation for the greater part of the modern world.

But are not three-quarters of our modern ills due to the fact that we have forgotten how to live, being unable or unwilling to allow ourselves time to relax? Yet in these uplands we have a people who still enjoy life. Neighbour to the wind and cloud and the wild birds of the moor, they can still find time to "stand and stare". Let a man from the lowlands go up amongst them and they will keep him talking for hours, so ready are they to enjoy a little of the more sociable, human pleasures of life. Surrounded by large stretches of lonely country, they accord due and proper recognition to the value of society, and out of this has arisen *y noson lawen*, and *y noswylio*, the talk by the hearth of a winter night. Go up into these solitudes, and pass by one of these small farms with the scent of the peat coming sweetly to you from the blackened chimney, and likely as not the goodman of the house, if he sees you, will come towards you for the sake of a few words, and after he has found out all about you with a disarming ingenuousness, you will probably be invited to drink a cup of tea with them in the kitchen. And on your departure you will meet a stray group of dark-eyed children, the girls in red skirts, making their way homeward from the distant school, that is often three miles away.

I know that these same people are but the shadows of what their fathers were, and yet their lives are more colourful and more interesting than the life of the average lowlander. In the lowlands they work all day, read little or nothing, and divide their leisure time between the markets and the cinemas. But here and there among the upland people there are poets, musicians, pennillion singers,and men possessed of a rare personality, who will pass into local tradition as *hen gymeriadau,* old characters. Only a year ago the last of the turf-roofed crofts became vacant owing to the subsidence of the main chimney. Two old men lived there at first; one died, but the other remained, half-blind though he was. The staircase leading to the loft where he slept was little better than a rickety ladder that swayed alarmingly as one trod it. The old man was scared out of his wits by the noise of the falling chimney, since he was unable to see what was happening. However, he would still have remained, had not a kindly neighbour taken him into her house and cared for him until his death about a year later at the age of eighty-three. He died having no English. A terrible condition for a Briton of the twentieth century? No, he was as merry and much more interesting than the crickets which sang to him from his hearth.

Then there is the poet who lives away out over the bog. I was sitting one day in the dry grasses reading some verse when he came up. "I often think," he said by way of greeting, "that there is more interest in the hills than anywhere else." He looked around over the empty moors and drew in a deep breath. "You can smell the sea to-day," he exclaimed. He began to recite a poem he had written about the searchlights during a raid on Merseyside. I looked up at him with the wide, blue air around him, and a strange emotion came over me. He was haloed with the clear light and his face was alive, his eyes keen. In his rough shirt-sleeves and his old cap he had all the beauty of a bog flower or a tree, or anything that had grown out of the grassy moor. And I realized very clearly that it was because he belonged there and was happy there.

Most of the people are good with their hands too. Apart from the traditional craft of cutting peat, much more difficult than it looks, many of them make their own implements, such as scythe or axe handles and wooden spoons. And then there is the man whose small stacks, thatched with reeds, are as primitively beautiful as a painting by Van Gogh.

Yes, there they are to be found still with their concerts and *eisteddfodau,* in winter, and their turf-cutting and harvesting in the summer. Their life is lived at a slower tempo than is comprehensible to this present age, for it takes a man hours to drive his cart over the boggy track to the nearest road to fetch a load of lime, or perhaps if it has been too wet for peat-gathering, a load of coal. And these are the people for whom something must be done.

We hear much talk of post-war development, and I believe there are plans for recultivating the uplands and running them from large lowland centres. But that is just what I deprecate, for it means the end of these people. No one who knows this district intimately, but can feel its wayward and carefree charm, but can realise that here still, however faintly, beats the old heart of Wales. That is why we are all Welsh Nationalists deep down within us, even if we do not subscribe outwardly to the policy of *Y Blaid*.

> I ninnau boed byw
> Yn ymyl gwisg Duw,
> Yn y grug, yn y grug.[1]

The land is sacred and the people who live close to it belong there and must be kept there, and some who have left it must be induced to return. It is useless to try to settle strangers there.

Certain efforts are being made, I know, to revive the country districts of Wales by encouraging small, rural industries, and that is all to the good. But that will hardly benefit or even touch the uplands. What we want there are good roads and grants or loans to put the houses and buildings in repair and a revival of the type of trade such as the wool trade, which would benefit these people. But the outer world is in chaos and the rule of the day is planning and uniformity, and small districts such as these are in danger of being completely overlooked owing to the more serious or spectacular nature of other problems. But unless something is done and done soon, official planning will go on, the desire for uniformity will proceed to its logical conclusion, and we shall have rows of monotonous cottages, with lorries to convey the workers up to the hills in the morning, and back at night, while one by one these hardy and extremely individual people, whose crofts blend so well with their environment, people who are attuned to the old, traditional life of the earth, who see every evening the sun go down over Cader Idris or Aran Mawddwy, and every summer the moor white with bog cotton, people who are the descendants of those most colourful rogues, *y gwylliaid Mawddwy*,[2] one by one, I say, will be allowed to die out or resort to a life in the towns or lowlands, a life which to them is no life at all, for they would be deracinés.

Notes
1. These lines reappear in R.S. Thomas's 'A Welsh View of the Scottish Renaissance', *Wales*, VIII:30 (1948), pp. 600-604. The author gives the following translation in the text of *The Mountains* (1968):

> But give us to live
> At the bright hem of God,
> In the heather, in the heather.

2. A reference to the bandits who were said to live in the vicinity of Dinas Mawddwy.

Some Contemporary Scottish Writing

Wales, VI:3 (1946), pp. 98-103

Some Contemporary Scottish Writing

Most of us should have become painfully aware by now of the difference in the attitudes of Scottish and Welsh M.P.s to questions concerning their respective countries. With the example of the vigour and unity of the former ministers fresh in my mind, it was, therefore, interesting to examine some Scottish writing which recently came my way. I wondered, naturally, whether the same unity and national consciousness would be apparent, or whether, like too many of our own writers, they would simply be limping along in the rear of Eliot, Auden, and company limited.

What I found was heartening, to say the least. To begin with there is behind the Scottish literary movement today a man of real stature, Hugh MacDiarmid, who exercises a stimulating influence upon his admirers, not only by his personal integrity, but also through his preference for Scots as a medium of poetic expression. Whatever one may have against Scots, such as its making the best of both worlds linguistically, one cannot overlook its many virtues, especially at a time when English is showing signs, not, as some people claim, of exhaustion, but of having reached the climacteric period of its life.

As a commentary on MacDiarmid's use of Scots, there are many lively passages in his autobiography, *Lucky Poet*, a quixotic book in a way, to use the word in Unamuno's sense. As one consistently antagonistic to English influences, it has been and still is MacDiarmid's task to de-anglicize Scotland, and so get back to the native roots. Naturally, therefore, his first preoccupation as a poet was with language. How well he succeeds can be realized at once from such lines as:

> There was nae reek i' the laverock's hoose
> That nicht—an' nane i' mine.[1]

Does not "laverock" awaken memories of what we used to call the bird before the stranger came with his superior lisp?

As a result of the new emphasis on national identity and the Scots dialect, we find also a fresh interest in other languages, and a revival of the traditional Scottish contact with France and the continent, so that some writers are as familiar with French, Russian or Spanish literature as they are with English. This bears rich fruit sometimes, as in Douglas Young's magnificent rendering of Valery's 'Le Cimitière Marin'. Listen to this:

> But i' their nicht, wechtit wi marble stane,
> a drowie fowk, down at the tree ruits lain,
> hae sideit wi you i slaw solemnitie.[2]

The word "drowie" takes us far back before the Saxon Invasion. And then there is this:

> Kittlit lassies' skreighans, blyth an keen
> bricht, whyte teeth, blue an greetan een,
> the loesome breist, whaur the reid lowelicht lay...

Does that not put one in mind of some of our *hen bennillion*?

> Nid oes rhyngof ac ef heno
> Onid pridd ac arch ac amdo;
> Mi fûm lawer gwaith ymhellach,
> Ond nid erioed â chalon drymach.[3]

Scots may be only a branch, but in such verse as this it is obvious that it is nourished by the main trunk of poetry, which grows century by century independently of towns and coteries and all the clap-trap of so called progressive writers. This is not to say that Scots is always successful. It is more fitted for some subjects than others, and can also be mawkishly sentimental, as MacDiarmid shows in a quotation from J.M.Barrie. But it has about it an air of fierceness which makes it peculiarly apt for the expression of *saeva indignatio*. Douglas Young's translation of Sorley Maclean's 'Heliant Woman', and these lines from 'Le Cimitière Marin':

> D'ye think ye'll sing when ye're a wraith o reek?
> C'wa! For aa thing flees! Frae pores I leak!
> And unco-guid Impatience tae maun dee!

suggests that power to upbraid, which made Raftery in Ireland and Twm o'r Nant in Wales poets to be feared by the unprincipled and mean.

Scots has, too, a braw quality in keeping with its environment which makes one wonder why in equally stern surroundings so much modern Welsh writing is jingling and sweet. There are people living under the harsh crags of Cader Idris and Yr Wyddfa, or on the bare gaunt moorland of central Wales, but their verse is tame to the point of lifelessness, The local papers are full of it every week. The eisteddfod adjudicators present them with rosettes year after year. Nor does this sort of thing confine itself to the Welsh writers. The *Western Mail* poetry column contains some pretty pieces in English, too. And that brings us to the case of MacDiarmid once more. His job was, he tells us himself, to "discredit and hustle off the stage a ... mawkish doggerel ... into which the Burns tradition had degenerated . . . rubbish without a single redeeming feature, by railwaymen poets, butcher poets, postmen poets, scavenger poets, policemen poets, and Heaven knows what else."[4]

The work of MacDiarmid's younger admirers and compatriots in familiarizing themselves with many tongues and a wide learning, whilst at the same time turning for inspiration to local material, is nothing less than a fulfilment of J.R.Lowell's requirement, "the tongue of the people in the mouth of the scholar." We have fulfilled that condition in Wales for many hundreds of years, but there are signs now that the mantle of writers like T. Gwynn Jones and W.J. Gruffydd is falling not upon the younger Welsh writers, but upon those of us who express ourselves in the English tongue. We must not grow heady with this new distinction, and forget that we also are Welshmen. Ireland has contrived to remain Irish despite her use of English, and there is no overwhelming reason why we should not succeed also, provided we can get rid of that foolish epithet, Anglo-Welsh.

On the other hand we must not make the mistake to which national literary movements are prone. One notices a tendency in Scottish as in Irish circles to stress the difference of the writing from the English tradition, whereas all too often it is simply a case of "the lady protests too much, methinks." One needs to take to heart the words of Seumas O'Sullivan in his review of *Poems from Ireland*. "Owing to the assiduity of commercial travellers and the absence of any serious literary publishers in this country, our bookshops are full of the latest London books of verse, and many of our younger Irish writers do not seem to have had the initiative to seek further than our shop windows.... The title *Poems from Ireland*, suggests that we have a commodity for export, but we can hardly re-import their own products to America and England."[5]

That is what I felt in reading verse by W.S.Graham, Ruthven Todd, George Bruce, and Archie Lamont. Todd has an epigrammatic style and international sympathies, Graham a large vocabulary, but there is, apart from certain local colour, or an occasional image or epithet, little to distinguish these poems from those by contemporary English writers. There is no need however to compare Graham unfavourably with Dylan Thomas, he is outdone in a typically metaphysical passage by the anglophobe, MacDiarmid. Take these lines fron the 'Fifth Journey', by Graham:

> Becoming the shame on a spilling virgin's mask
> My limbs erect a hovering roof of birds
> To shelter this unfenced river-couch of dams
> Where gardeners prune the glow-worm coasts in breasts
> And screen her vault's vagina with tormenting rakes.

and set beside them these from Hugh MacDiarmid's 'Harry Semen':

> Grey ghastly commentaries on my puir life,
> A' the sperm that's gane for naething rises up to dam
> In sick-white onanism the single seed
> Frae which in sheer irrelevance I cam.
> What were the odds against me? Let me coont.
> What worth am I to a' that micht ha'e been?
> To a' the wasted slime I'm capable o
> Appeals this lurid emission, whirlin lint-white and green.

Archie Lamont for all his use of local names and occasional Scots fails to make his verse resound with the passion which Yeats breathed into similar metres. The feeling is genuine, but is the patriotism of the scholar rather than the poet.

William Soutar and Edwin Muir are in a different category. Soutar wrote in Scots and English, but no doubt as a result of his being bedridden, his poems are more personal and reflective, and manifest a preoccupation with the spiritual struggle against pain and evil. Edwin Muir, a well-known critic, writes distinguished verse of a higher standard than most of that produced by the nationalist poets, but decidedly in the manner of English philosophical poetry.

An interesting poet in virtue of his English tongue wedded to a pronouncedly Scottish style and sympathy is Adam Drinam. Most of his verse relies on vivid representation of the highland landscape, but he is capable of many an original and striking image. "Will not the wind stop lowing about the house?" and "Christ, the silver salmon, dead in dark blue window glass," are typical quotations from his latest book, *Women of the Happy Island*. But although this shows an advance in thought content, I preferred his earlier volume, *Men of the Rocks*. However, Drinam's greatest achievement as far as I am concerned is his success in conveying an unmistakeably Scottish atmosphere by means of the English tongue. I cannot yet see how we Welsh poets writing in English are to surmount the fact that much of our environment bears names which are irreducible to English, such as *bwlch*, *cwm*, *talar*, and so on, but a man like Drinam shows us how to begin.

For our own part the best thing that we younger poets can do is to follow Saunders Lewis' advice and read more of the typical Welsh writers like Emrys ap Iwan. For all we know, our movement may simply be a phase in the re-cymrification of Wales. What of it? The same thing is being aimed at in Ireland and Scotland. There are two considerable poets in Scotland who write exclusively in the Gaelic tongue. George Campbell Hay I am, unfortunately, unable to read, but Sorley Maclean appends a rough English translation to his work. That these men are no romantic reactionaries can be seen from lines such as the following from Sorley Maclean, translated by Douglas Young:

> My een are nae on Calvary
> Or the Bethlehem they praise,
> But on shitten back-lands in Glesga toun
> Whaur growan life decays,
> And a stairheid room in an Embro land,
> A chalmer o puirtith and skaith,
> Whaur monie a shilpet bairnikie
> Gaes smoorit doun til daith.[6]

It is heartening, therefore, to find two poets at least who, whilst being fully alive to the present situation, have yet found that they can best express themselves in the old language of their people. Is so old and pure a language as Welsh to fail where Gaelic succeeds? With some fearless and imaginative work by men such as Professor Ifor Williams, there is no reason why the deficiencies in modern

Welsh should not be made good and a vigorous and pliable medium handed on to posterity, purified of all English phrases, catchwords, and such like. If only more Welshmen would read some of the older writers like Emrys ap Iwan and Theophilus Evans, we would have less of that limping or stilted Welsh which is a mere translation of an English idiom, and if those of us who write in English would read more widely among such men as Dafydd ap Gwilym, Tudor Aled, and Goronwy Owen, as well as paying more attention to the discipline of the strict metres, our work might begin to show some difference from that of the essentially urban-minded English poets who write for the most part in a highly sophisticated manner and with a consistently town outlook.

Of course, we must be honest. The muse is not to be browbeaten into singing an accompaniment to an ideology. We have ample proof of that not only in the work of some of the London political poets, like Julian Symons, but in that of John Singer, whose book, *The Fury of the Living*, is a peculiar mixture of Whitmanesque and traditional verse, interspersed with occasional pieces of a more individual and moving quality. But if communism is not sufficient in itself to lift verse to the level of poetry, neither is nationalism, which in a way is only the communism which begins at home. We must beware of lauding work merely because it has a national flavour. Poetry can still be bad poetry for all its tang. Whatever we mean by good poetry, we are agreed that it always possesses the "richt, authentic tone", and until we have cleared away a great deal of the rubbish in which we are as a generation bogged fast, until we have rinsed our eyes in a clear Welsh stream, and rid our ears of the continual, monotonous drone of modern propaganda, we shall continue in our aimless cacophony. What is the "richt, authentic tone"? MacDiarmid tells us himself:

> Hark! hark! 'tis the true, the joyful sound,
> Caoilte's shrill, round whistle over the brae,
> The freeing once more of the winter-locked ground...[7]

And so we come full circle back to the crude reality, the necessity for politics, distasteful as they may appear. For it is England, the home of the industrial revolution, and the consequent twentieth-century rationalism, that have been the winter on our native pastures, and we must break their grip, and the grip of all the quislings and yes-men before we can strike that authentic note. When the national soul is in danger, when, in the words of William Power, it is a case of "choosing between national extinction and an enlargement of national consciousness" what poet can luxuriate in the privacy of his own lyrical garden? Has not Saunders Lewis deliberately left unfulfilled his early promise as a poet in order to try to avert that national extinction? In a short poem Hugh MacDiarmid also tells us why he became a nationalist:

> Like Pushkin, I,
> My time for flichty conquests by,
> Valuing nae mair some quick-fire cratur
> Wha hurries up the ways o' natur'
> Am happy, when after lang and sair
> Pursuit you yield yoursel' to me...[8]

Before the awful levelling process of modern uniformity and centralization, the cultivation of one's own poetic individuality, however integrating to the personality, however charming to a few admirers, is a sign of the failure to grow up and begin the wooing of a more exacting lover.

In order to prepare himself for the task of clearing the ground in his own country, every Welshman should read *Lucky Poet*. Let him substitute in almost every case the word "Wales" for "Scotland" and the revelation will be shattering. MacDiarmid is an indomitable fighter. He is not to be daunted by the attacks of the enemy, be they insidious or ruthless. To him the English are parvenu when compared with the great antiquity of Gaelic Scotland. The English are west Europeans, therefore anything as un-European as Scottish pibroch or Welsh *penillion* singing is anathema to them. Most British history in the English tongue is traced from the Roman period onwards, and this conception of England as the cradle of British civilization has been gradually foisted upon the Cymric and Gaelic peoples, and until recently was rarely questioned. But now a new Don Quixote has arisen in Scotland to break a lance with the all-pervading twentieth-century rationalism that goes hand in hand with western democracy and industrial development. Perhaps it would hearten him to know that his good servant, Sancho Panza, keeps up the fight in Wales against the same enemy. I refer to *Y Faner*,[9] which week after week endeavours to re-awaken the half-stifled patriotism of our country. In this connection too, especially stimulating is MacDiarmid's quotation from Professor Brie of

Freiburg University. Doctor Brie distinguishes between two kinds of
patriotism, the offensive and the defensive, assigning the former to
England, and the latter to Scotland. To quote Brie's own words: "In
the nature of things the defensive, by its closer connection with
ethical ideas, contains the greater potentialities, while the offensive
too easily squanders itself in boasts about its own virtues and insults
to its opponents." [10]

But like a true prophet MacDiarmid does not direct his wrath
solely or even mainly against other nations. He may record his
recreation in *Who's Who* as anglophobia, but it is the quislings and
lickspittles in his own country that are his chief enemies. On this
subject too, there is a moving novel by Fionn MacColla, called *And
the Cock Crew*, which deals mainly with the Highland clearances of
the eighteenth-century, but has contemporary implications, when
we remember that at the present time the last of the crofters are
being sacrificed on the altar of industrial progress and commercial
enterprise. The book is also valuable to us Welsh people in its
portrayal of Calvinism's paralysing effect on the will of the
Highlanders to active resistance.

MacDiarmid is especially fierce with that unimaginative,
bourgeois element, which forms so large a proportion of present day
Scotland. William Power describes his attitude in these words:
"MacDiarmid's nationalism arose out of anger at the domination of
public life in Scotland by uncultured third-raters, ignorant of their
own country's history and literature, and hanging on to the coat-
tails of England. His fulminations have been directed against people
who in some way were preventing Scotland's full expression of the
best that was in her. He wants to see Scotland 'respected like the
lave,' not for her ships and engines, banks and investment
companies, prize bulls and sporting estates, Empire-builders and
'heids o' depairtments'; not even for her kirks and her Sabbath; but
for her intellect and art, her developed national culture, her social
justice and equity."

This reminds us of that large body of Welsh people, whose sole
criterion of success is appointment to some post under the English
government; who have willingly surrendered their age-old customs
and traditions for the bric a brac of a bourgeois existence in houses
indistinguishable from English suburbia. Gone is the pride of race
that produced lines such as those by Huw Dafi, when his master
talked of making an English marriage:

> Pa les o daw Saesnes hir
> I baradwys ein brodir?
> Ni charaf, anaf unoed
> Gwys o'r iaith gasa' erioed...
> Cymer ferch Cymro farchawg
> Aur i gyd i war a'i gawg.
> Cais ferch addfain ugainmlwydd
> Ac na chais ferch Sais o'r swydd.[11]

It is against the English conception of Scotland, a one-sided view down to which generations of Scots have been levelled, a view fostered and supported by directors of education and the capitalist press, a Scotland of "chortling wut", that MacDiarmid is fighting, and it is against a similar conception of Wales that we should take up arms. What is Wales to England after all but a kind of western county that is not worth bothering about apart from its scenery and its natural resources? Wild Wales! Yes, but it all resides in the landscape. The true character of modern Wales is that she is a peace-loving country, as witness her sincere support of the League of Nations. But the pill of conscription has been sugared by reports in the press of what Field Marshal Montgomery thought of his Welsh troops, and now for being such loyal subjects of the English government we are to have not the power to govern ourselves, not a square deal for Welsh home industries and agriculture, but a visit from the over-worked King and Queen, with a rapid muster of the few remaining harpers and a couple of Welsh costumes borrowed from some amateur dramatic society. And all the time in Wales, as in Scotland, the essential spirit of our people, a "spirit profoundly alien to that of England" hides itself far down in the depths of the personality, overlaid by generations of alien influence, productive of those inhibitions so common in our folk, yet waiting, waiting for the leaders who are great and fearless enough to awaken it to that "enlargement of national consciousness" already referred to.

This, then, is the key truth of MacDiarmid's work as a poet: "To bring to bear a material imagination on everyday reality, so as to emphasise the beauty which it possesses normally and in use. There is in this perception of beauty less magic and less exaltation than in that of romantic poetry, but on the other hand it has more toughness, vigour and fulness. The romantic note is, of course, often heard in Scottish poetry, but it is this other note that is essentially Scottish."

The reader may think that I am now confusing his literary with
his political aims, but if we subscribe to Shelley's description of the
poet as the unacknowledged legislator, then it is only by upholding
such an ideal in poetry that we can at long last change the people and
lead them to their essential dignity. It is because that dignity, that
personality, that soul is so different, even alien in the Celtic peoples,
that it has aroused the unfailing antagonism of generation after
generation of English official classes and their quisling admirers.

It is a formidable task this winnowing and purifying of the people,
because it so nearly forms a vicious circle. There can be no national
art without a people, and there can be no people without artists to
create them and give form to their dreams and aspirations. This
seems to me the crux of the matter. The poet's chief problem is, how
in virtue of his mind and vision can he best save his country—
directly through political action, or indirectly through his creative
work? Failure to resolve this difficulty leads to frustration and
inertia. There, too, is the dilemma of the so-called Anglo-Welsh
writers. They are the new generation, the product of the new age.
Are they, then, to be the instruments of the final capitulation of their
country, or of "an enlargement of national consciousness"? And if
of the latter, how best can they achieve it, directly through political
action, or indirectly through a literary movement? And what is to be
the permanent language of such a movement? We have to face the
possibility not, I think, of the disappearance of Welsh, but of its
inadequacy   as   a   medium   for   expressing   the   complex
phantasmagoria of modern life. But if we choose English as that
medium, have we the singleness of mind, the strength of will to
remain primarily Welshmen? Ireland has done it, Scotland is
striving after it, and we should do the same, for as MacDiarmid
affirms, unlike England, who has now nothing but a proletariat
anxious only for the "panis et circenses", Scotland, Ireland and
Wales are still a people, "a people full of remoteness, uncertainty
and hope", as he would see them, a timeless folk like those of Spain,
"who saw unexhausted Romans, Visigoths, Moors, Napolean".[12]

Perhaps owing to the over-towering stature and genius of one
man, this has been a rather one-sided review of some contemporary
literature. Let me, then, mention briefly a few other interesting
features of cultural life in Scotland at the present time. MacDiarmid
himself runs a virile magazine, called *The Voice of Scotland*. Then,
also, the movement has the enviable advantage of a publishing firm

sympathetic to its cause. William McLellan has published most of the writers of the Scottish Renaissance group in a series of cheap volumes, together with a book of Gaelic poetry by Sorley Maclean. Besides this the firm also publishes two journals, *Poetry Scotland*, and *Scottish Art and Letters*, which provide a platform for free and lively discussion of the various aspects of a national economy and a new realization of separate individuality, with their consequent demand for independence.

Judging by the cover designs and illustrations to some of these works, Scottish plastic art would appear to be in a less healthy condition. Most of the reproductions seem to be mere pastiche, either upon early Scottish designs, or on modern English and continental post-surrealism. What are more admirable are the recitals of contemporary Scottish music, together with poetry readings, organised by the Dunedin Association for the encouragement of the Scottish creative arts.[13] What have we in Wales to compare with this? Certainly not the C.E.M.A.[14] A lecture recital of pibroch by F.G.Scott and James Barke, for instance, reminds one of the danger in which Welsh folk music stands. It seems that genuine Welsh folk song exists largely as an oral tradition now, and is more than likely to pass away with its present exponents. Those of us who have been privileged to hear people like Miss Cassi Davies rendering an old Welsh folk song, cannot but wish that we, too, had some equivalent to the Dunedin Association which would preserve and encourage the art of folk and penillion singing, as well as afford a platform to our neglected composers like Morgan Nicholas, E.T.Davies, and Bradwen Jones.

All in all, then, allowing for the inclusion of work that is less originally Scottish, or of a somewhat lower standard, recent Scottish art, as seen in this short survey—which, of course, passes over established writers as Neil Gunn, Compton Mackenzie, and Eric Linklater—affords more hope for the future than does that of Wales, where, as Seumas O'Sullivan has said, ''the possibility of a definite Welsh literary movement becomes less, as interests multiply and aims become confused.''

Notes
1. From MacDiarmid's 'The Watergaw'.
2. These and the following lines are from Douglas Young's 'The Kirkyaird by the Sea' which was later selected by R.S.Thomas to appear in his edition of *The Penguin Book of Religious Verse* (1963).

3. This verse appears in *The Oxford Book of Welsh Verse*, ed. Thomas Parry (O.U.P., 1962), no.151: "There is only earth, a coffin and a shroud between me and him tonight; I have been further many times, but never with such a heavy heart".
4. From 'The Kind of Poetry I Want', chapter 3 of *Lucky Poet* (Methuen: London, 1943).
5. Seumas O'Sullivan was at that time editor of *The Dublin Magazine*. His review of *Poems from Ireland* appeared in *The Dublin Magazine*, XX:2 (1945), pp. 53-54.
6. This is a translation of Sorley Maclean's 'Calbharaigh'.
7. From MacDiarmid's 'The Gaelic Muse'.
8. From MacDiarmid's 'Why I Became a Nationalist'.
9. A weekly, Welsh-language publication, established in 1843 under the title *Baner ac Amserau Cymru*.
10. Quoted by MacDiarmid in 'The Ideas Behind My Work', chapter 6 of *Lucky Poet* (Methuen: London, 1943).
11. A lanky limb of an Englishwoman here
    in this paradise of our brothers? To what end?
    Nor do I like (it hurts just the same)
    her cursed language, the worst under the sun.
    Come, choose the daughter of a Welsh knight,
    gold up to his chin and his plate gold, too.
    Take as your wife one of our slim twenty-year olds,
    and not the offspring of a paid English official.
                    (translated by R.S.Thomas)
12. MacDiarmid expands these ideas in 'The Kind of Poetry I Want', chapter 3 of *Lucky Poet* (Methuen: London, 1943).
13. The Dunedin Association is more properly known as the Dunedin Society. The substance of an address entitled 'A Welsh View of the Scottish Renaissance', that R.S.Thomas delivered to this Society, was printed in *Wales*, VIII:30 (1948), pp. 600-604.
14. The Council for the Encouragement of Music and the Arts was established in 1940.

Dau Gapel

Y Fflam, 5 (1948), pp. 7-10

[Two Chapels]

Two Chapels

It is strange, I suppose, for a Churchman like myself to have chosen such a subject, but what else could I do being so fond of the Welsh countryside? In Wales you find very few churches situated in lonely out-of-the-way places but I have come across many small chapels in wild romantic settings, a sign, I suppose, of the adventurous spirit of the early nonconformists. But I'm afraid by today it is quite a different story: the chapels, like the churches, are in retreat. What has become of the pioneering spirit of the early saints who founded monastries and oratories in places that are now uninhabited? Consider Bardsey Island for instance. Why won't the church send a priest to celebrate Holy Communion there and preach the Gospel to its inhabitants? I must admit that, generally speaking, it is the Chapels and not the Churches that try to feed the flock in Wales, and by flock, I mean the scattered ones.

Last summer I went to visit—among other things—two chapels, one in Radnorshire and the other in Cardiganshire. Both of them were remote but this was the only thing they had in common. One was much older than the other and the atmosphere of the two differed completely. I am going to call the first "The Chapel of the Spirit" and the second "The Chapel of the Soul", not because the worshippers perceive them as such but because they so appear to me.

Maes-yr-Onnen is the name of the first. It stands on high ground overlooking the river Wye as it winds its way towards England. I went there on a sunny morning in August with the East wind

chasing the clouds across the blue sky. When I had walked around
the building and stared in through the windows (there was no one
there to unlock the door for me), I stretched myself out on the grass
and let my mind wander back into the past. And indeed after a
while, I saw the first worshippers coming through the fields—sober
men and women dressed in a sober fashion. I saw them leave the
sunlight for the darkness of the chapel and then heard the rustling of
the Bible pages and the murmurs of soft voices mingling with the
wind. Yes, it was two and a half centuries earlier on a fine August
morning. And almost immediately, I saw, I understood. As with St.
John the Divine on the island of Patmos I was "in the Spirit" and I
had a vision, in which I could comprehend the breadth and length
and depth and height of the mystery of the creation. But I won't try
to put the experience into words. It would be impossible. I will
simply say that I realised there was really no such thing as time, no
beginning and no end but that everything is a fountain welling up
endlessly from immortal God. There was certainly something in the
place that gave me this feeling. The chapel stood in the fields, amidst
the waving grass, its roof covered with a layer of yellow lichen.
There were tall nettles growing around and at its side there swayed a
big old tree like someone leaning forward to listen to the sermon. It
was therefore easy to believe that I was living centuries ago. It might
have been the first day of Creation and myself one of the first men.
Might have been? No it *was* the first day. The world was recreated
before my eyes. The dew of its creation was on everything, and I fell
to my knees and praised God—a young man worshipping a young
God, for surely that is what our God is.

Duw ieuanc ydyw Duw: Duw'r gwanwyn clir...[1]

Why, I wonder, when we think of the past do we tend to see it as if at
the end of a corridor with the result that we get an impression of
darkness. And why do we refer to the "old days" as if we had finally
climbed up into a new world. To quote from Gwili again:

Nid ydw Natur fawr yn mynd yn hen...[2]

Yes, there was sunshine and summer in the land when Branwen
walked by the river Alaw in Anglesey. Glyndŵr too saw the shadow
of the clouds fleeing before the east wind; and the first worshippers
in Maes-yr-Onnen heard the cry of the buzzard above them as I
heard it more than two centuries later. It therefore seems to me

MAES YR ONNEN   Elsie Thomas

vain—in more than one sense of the word—to go on about the "dark ages". Maes yr Onnen chapel *is* the Chapel of the Spirit.

A few days later I was gazing at the other chapel—Soar-y-Mynydd—where it shelters behind a row of copper beeches.

How different everything was here! Even though it was still August, the weather was cold and cloudy and the only sounds to break the silence were the thin, complaining voice of the stream and the constant drip of moisture from the trees. If the wind gasped once, it immediately fell silent, as if afraid of its own voice. There was no-one in the chapel nor in the adjoining house. In fact there was no sign of life at all, apart from the odd sheep on the hill-pastures nearby. Yet everything about the place showed it was well kept. The windows were clean, the walls were of a pleasant colour, and there was a row of white stones around every flower-bed. This was a chapel, then, for the scattered community of people who would travel once a week from their hidden inaccessible homes, to worship and pray together for a short time, and then home they would go, each along his own particular path on his frisky pony, sunk in long and deep meditation.

SOAR Y MYNYDD   Elsie Thomas

Soar-y-Mynydd is a very different place from the other chapel as I
have already mentioned; but here, too, I had a vision. In Maes-yr-
Onnen I had a glimpse of the spirit of man; here, I saw the soul of a
special type of man, the Cymro or Welshman. For the very source of
Welsh life as it is today is here in the middle of these remote
moorlands of Ceredigion. And it is in places of this sort that the soul
of the true Welshman is formed.

If I had to choose between the two chapels, I would no doubt
prefer the second. Because I am only human? Because of the
weakness of the flesh? I don't know. All I know is that I also visited
Ireland last summer, and happened to go to hear mass in a Roman
Catholic church. The longing that came over me there was a longing
for some small chapel like this in the Welsh hills, with its small
congregation of sober down-to-earth people.

What, then is the purpose of this rambling essay? It is an attempt
to describe what Wales means to me, and also to discover the true
soul of my people. Speaking of denominations, I must admit that
Noncomformity still wins hands down. The formal ostentation of
Catholicism won't do here. And the Church in Wales isn't any

longer Welsh enough in Spirit. But there is something else to be said. I haven't much to say to mysticism and other-worldliness; this is obvious from my choice of Soar-y-Mynydd rather than Maes-yr-Onnen. Nor, in my opinion, do these things appeal to the Welsh as a nation either. I am always ready to admit the value of the spirit, but how often do we hear today of the spiritual as something opposed to ideas of nationalism and so on. The truth is that a nation that is fighting for survival cannot afford to change its soul for some obscure spirituality no matter how excellent that may be from the individual's point of view. Anyone who can feel for the life of the Welsh countryside has experienced something too strong and too profound to be ascribed to another world, or another life. Here, in the soil and the dirt and the peat do we find life and heaven and hell, and it is in these surroundings that a Welshman should forge his soul. When the Welsh as a nation were bound to this kind of life, then their souls were strong and deep. In the towns, especially the towns in England, what else awaits you but the spiritual? But towns are not characteristic of Wales; they are evidence of foreign influence, and the sooner they disappear the better.

Notes
1. From John Gwili Jenkins (Gwili) 'Natur a Duw': "God is a young God: the God of the fresh Spring".
2. *Ibid.*: "Great nature does not grow old".

Llenyddiaeth Eingl-Gymreig

Y Fflam, 11 (1952), pp.7-9

[Anglo-Welsh Literature]

Anglo-Welsh Literature

Sometimes someone coins a term, and then, for good or ill, we have to consider the phenomenon to which that term refers. I do not know who is responsible for the term "the Anglo-Welsh", but there can be no doubt that such a school of writers exists. We therefore have to assess their contribution.

The first thing that strikes us is the lack of agreement about the meaning of the term "Anglo-Welsh literature". What is it? Literature by Welsh people about Welsh things? Literature by English people about Wales? Or literature by Welsh people about any subject at all? We have examples of all three in the work of men such as Caradoc Evans, Thomas Love Peacock and Vernon Watkins. One can, no doubt, group such writers together to make a "school" but the sum of their contributions does not necessarily create a literature with a feel of its own to it.

The fact is that if we want to get hold of the true meaning of the term "English-language Welsh literature" we had much better approach the matter from another direction. Let us consider two views of the Welsh tradition as given by two scholars, namely Matthew Arnold and Sir Idris Bell.

You will remember that Arnold in his book *Celtic Literature* ascribes some of the style and melancholy of English literature, and all of its magic to a Celtic origin; and one may well be able to find examples of these things even among the Welsh who have written in English, for Henry Vaughan has style and Edward Thomas melancholy, and there is no lack of magic in the work of Manley Hopkins and Dylan

Thomas. But these features are not more characteristic of the literature of the Welsh than of other peoples. I feel that Sir Idris Bell is closer to the mark when he describes the chief characteristics of Welsh literature as "a feeling for discipline; a love of clear, concise and elegant phrasing; a force and precision of utterance." In this context it is also interesting to note what a reviewer in the *Times Literary Supplement* once said about a collection of stories and poems: "There is a strong Welsh element in the book, which accounts for much of its murkiness." One can easily see how this may come about if Arnold's view is taken as the model. And unfortunately, the way the world is today, with its emphasis on what will sell and on offering the reader escape, there is more room for those who follow Arnold than for those who admire Bell. The majority of publishers and booksellers are for ever urging writers to produce something that is "different", and this is what accounts for the vogue of the Anglo-Irish, the Anglo-Scots and the Anglo-Welsh. But the picture of their countries given by these writers is far from accurate, and as a result serious artists protest that the muse should not be violated in this way, since the true artist needs freedom. Other things being equal, there is a great deal to be said for such a view, but what shall we say of this attitude in a country in such a pitiful condition as Wales is? Perhaps it is *possible*, even in Wales, for an artist to create whatever he wants to, but is it *right*? That is what some of the English-speaking Welsh have forgotten in seeking to satisfy only the English. They have sinned against their own nation. It would not be fair to name anyone in particular, but there are many examples.

But it is worth observing that England has a name even for that third category of writers, those who try to remain faithful to their own tradition. "Regionalism" is the word—the London word for the writers who are brave enough and able enough to ignore the influence of the Leviathan. And even T.S.Eliot accepts the word and takes for granted the right of English literature to benefit from the activity of the various "regions". What is this but another name for "blood transfusion"? The ageing body of English literature will stave off death so long as new blood continues to flow into it. From where have the chief influences of English literature come over the last half-century if not from men such as James Joyce in prose, and Manley Hopkins, Edward Thomas, Wilfred Owen and Dylan Thomas in poetry—the first an Irishman, and the others all Welsh? The tragedy for the Welsh-language culture is that these writers have had to write in English, indeed one must say in fairness to them that the majority of the Anglo-Welsh school write in English not by whim but from necessity. We have been deprived of our heritage.

What can we do then? My view is this: since there is in Wales a mother-tongue that continues to flourish, a proper Welshman can only look on English as a means of rekindling interest in the Welsh-language culture, and of leading people back to the mother-tongue. We need, therefore, to aim consistently at this objective, remembering Whitman's words in his song 'By Blue Ontario Shore': "Who are you, indeed, who would talk or sing to America? Have you studied out the land, its idioms and men? Have you learned the physiology, phrenology, politics, geography, pride, freedom, friendship of the land?" The signs of having done this are too scarce in the work of the majority of the English-language Welsh. For one thing, too many of them come from the industrial areas. They tend therefore to give an unbalanced picture of Wales, creating the impression that it is a land of coal-mines. But to me, the true Wales is still to be found in the country. The heavy industries came from outside and are something new: but the country tradition runs back across the centuries as something essentially Welsh, and every Welsh writer whatever his language, has a responsibility in this respect. He should work for the continuance of this tradition, for who knows but that the future will once more belong to small countries.

That is the first duty of the Anglo-Welsh. And secondly they should aim at creating a literature that is more compatible with the literary tradition in Welsh by giving more attention to those features which Sir Idris Bell notes as characteristic of the Welsh muse. For example, greater attention to the study of *cynghanedd*[1] would bring discipline to their work, and the clarity which Bell praised would teach them to be more honest in their depiction of Wales.

Note
1. A system of alliteration or consonance in a line of Welsh poetry in strict metre.

The Qualities of Christmas

Wales, 46 (1959), pp. 17-20

The Qualities of Christmas

"In the juvescence of the year came Christ the tiger", wrote Mr T.S. Eliot in *Gerontion* with history and metaphysics at his elbow.

> It was the winter wild
> While the Heaven-born child
> All meanly wrapped in the rude manger lies...

So sang John Milton in the 'Hymn of the Morning of Christ's Nativity' with less historical accuracy perhaps, but more in keeping with our northern sensibility. There is something oriental about Mr Eliot's line; a sense of dryness and savagery, recalling the season when the planet Mars burns ominously in the eastern sky. But in Milton's stanza there is a note of the carol: "In the bleak mid-winter, frosty wind made moan". It brings that sense of coldness and crispness which has become the conventional environment of an English Christmas. How many children and grown-ups feel a secret desire for snow, or at least a touch of frost on Christmas Eve? The very word Christ has that thin, crisp sound so suggestive of frost and snow and the small sheets of ice that crack and splinter under our feet, even as the Host is broken in the priest's fingers.

Christianity has tended to be transformed or adapted in every country into which it has made its way. Perhaps the saddest transformation here has been its increasing commercialization: the rush, the false gaiety, the perfunctory exchange of cards and presents; the colossal expenditure of energy and cash on the wrong things. But the subtlest influence remains climatic; and afterwards economic. Our more temperate winters afford a dual approach. We can relish the coldness of the season, the red cheeks, the high blood, without becoming insensitive to the claims of the hungry bird at our window, the pathos of bare boughs, and the darker associations of red berries in the snow. Also our economic prosperity over many centuries built up a feeling of snugness and warmth and good cheer within. "Fire and sleet and candlelight"—these lend zest to Christmas indoors in a comfortable home, without blinding us to the plight of the less fortunate without, those who are caught in "the cauld, cauld blast".

But there is something more. Christ was born in Bethlehem. Bethlehem was a town. But all around lay the country. This was the glory of the earlier towns. "The dark, satanic mills" had not arrived. The country came up to the town walls, as is so evident in the paintings of the mediaeval and renaissance masters. The place where Jesus was born was used as a cow byre. The creatures were there with their hay-sweet breath and their smell of the earth. And all around there was the country. St. Luke tells us: "And in the same country there were shepherds abiding in the field, keeping watch over their flock by night". "Abiding in the field". What a sense of the surrounding country we get in those words! It is this sense of the harmony of town and country which is so much part of the Nativity. Mary, like a farm wife, comes into the town to give birth to her child. The town that is the summit of man's achievement, the city that he builds to the glory of God. And the shepherds come in from the fields to see this great·wonder that has occurred, symbols of that flowing in of food and inspiration and re-invigoration without which all towns must wither and die. And there they find Christ, a sign of God's blessing upon the town as the focus of civilization; the place where the raw material of nature, of the country districts around, is transformed into those higher things which are for the benefit and enrichment of all.

It should be so here and now. Despite our many towns and cities, we are country folk at heart. This is still a green island. Our memories of Christmas, our experiences of it, are country ones. If we cannot get to the country for Christmas, we import it into our homes. We hang up holly and mistletoe. We arrange flowers and ivy and yew. We bear in the Christmas tree and make it grow again in our houses. We bring out our store of nuts and apples, and dine off game and poultry that but a few days earlier were on a Scottish moor or a Welsh hillside. These are reminders of the country around, that abiding wildness and freshness, where the strange stillness and hush of Christmas Eve can best be appreciated.

I remember one Christmas Eve; I think it was in 1941. There were rumours that the Germans would attempt an airborne landing that night. The countryside where I lived was wrapped in a thick, damp fog. The lanes were empty. No lights shone from the scattered farmsteads. The trees loomed up, windless and eerie, in the darkness. The silence was terrifying, the suspense intolerable. But it was suspense for the wrong thing. On other Christmas Eves I have walked up hill lanes to take a present of home-made cakes to a bedridden farmer. But how different the atmosphere! The air cold and clear, the ash trees bone-white against the sky. A friendly stream of warm light flowing from the farm window, and above, the shrill harness of the stars. And if a fox barked, it was a merry sound, for on such a Christmas Eve one could believe with Thomas Hardy's peasant in 'The Oxen' that all the beasts were kneeling.

> Christmas Eve, and twelve of the clock
> "Now they are all on their knees"

Hardy ends his poem on a characteristic note, half cynical, half wistful:

> I should go with him in the gloom,
> Hoping it might be so.

"Hoping it might be so"! But it is so.

Introduction to

The Penguin Book of religious Verse

(Penguin: Harmondsworth, 1963), pp. 7-11

Introduction to
The Penguin Book of Religious Verse

I must explain this anthology; first of all what it is not. It is not
chronological, nor is it a comprehensive survey of the field. Space
prevented the latter. The publishers felt that chronological sequence
can militate against effective juxtaposition of different authors or
passages. I agree. They felt, too, that the emphasis should be on the
quality of the poetry. I agree again, but do not wish my choice to
appear too definitive. The fact that Blake is represented by only one
poem and Byron by seven poems or extracts does not at all mean I
consider the latter a better poet than the former. But having
dispensed with chronological order, it was necessary that I should
have a theme. It is mainly in pursuance of this theme that I have
made my choice. But more of that later.

There are other omissions. In an anthology for the general reader
it did not seem feasible to include earlier English poetry. This
excluded Langland among others. Then there is the question of
translations. Very rarely, in my opinion, does a translation convey
the full quality of the original poem. Consequently, with the
exception of Douglas Young's magnificent rendering of Valéry, I
have omitted them. The Scots of Henryson and Dunbar, Young and
MacDiarmid, seemed far more intelligible to the average reader
than the English of Langland; hence their inclusion.

Since the anthology was not meant to be comprehensive, and
since the emphasis was to be on the quality of the verse, I have
omitted several poets who hold an established place in English
literature. It is here that the anthology will come under fire from the
various schools of thought. But on this point, despite the fact that it
is an anthology of *religious* verse, I must remain unrepentant. That

is, although I do not wish for too serious an interpretation of my omissions, it could be inferred from their absence that admittedly religious poets like Crashaw have not moved me much. On the other hand, I might not wish such an inference to be made in respect of another absentee, Traherne; which merely goes to show, perhaps, the knots in which an anthologist can tie himself!

This is a collection of poetry with a compound title, and like Plato's charioteer in the *Phaedrus* I feel I have an ill-assorted pair of horses bridled together. Religion? Yes. Verse? Yes. But with the increasing secularization of life, neither is very tolerant of the other. The more active animosity of religion, especially of Christianity, is of long standing. From the days of Tertullian, at least, there has been distrust of the aesthetic. It might not be too much to say that only now, in the middle of the present century, is a welcome broadening of approach at last apparent. And yet, turning to poetry, we find the concern is not with its lack of rapport with religion so much as with life itself. Poetry still has little hold over contemporary society.

What is the common ground between religion and poetry? Is there such? Do definitions help? If I say that religion is the total response of the whole person to reality, but poetry the response of a certain kind of person, I appear to be doing so at the expense of poetry. Perhaps Coleridge can help here. The nearest we approach to God, he appears to say, is as creative beings. The poet by echoing the primary imagination, recreates. Through his work he forces those who read him to do the same, thus bringing them nearer the primary imagination themselves, and so, in a way, nearer to the actual being of God as displayed in action. So Coleridge in the thirteenth Chapter of his *Biographia Literaria*. Now the power of the imagination is a unifying power, hence the force of metaphor; and the poet is the supreme manipulator of metaphor. This would dispose of the idea of him as a minor craftsman among many. The world needs the unifying power of the imagination. The two things which give it best are poetry and religion. Science destroys as it gives.

This anthology is divided into five sections. Roughly defining religion as embracing an experience of ultimate reality, and poetry as the imaginative presentation of such, I have considered five aspects of that experience: the consciousness of God, of the self, of negation, of the impersonal or un-nameable, and of completion. The first section takes us to the heart of the traditional religious experience: the confrontation with God, and God as personal. This is not an anthology of Christian verse. Would it have been narrower so? The sections are all from British and American poetry, but had I embraced Europe as a whole, it would have been seen still that the main fact in the religious consciousness of western man is the Judaeo-Christian revelation. The need for revelation at all suggests an ultimate reality beyond human attainment, the *mysterium tremendum et fascinans*. And here, surely, is common ground between religion and poetry. But there is the question of the mystic. To him the *Deus absconditus* is immediate; to the poet He is mediated. The mystic fails to mediate God adequately insofar as he is not a poet. The poet, with possibly less immediacy of apprehension, shows his spiritual concern and his spiritual nature through the medium of language, the supreme symbol. The presentation of religious experience in the most inspired language is poetry. This is not a definition of poetry, but a description of how the communication of religious experience best operates. Yet it is some of the poems in this book, which purport to do this, that will arouse the indignation of the religious, more especially of the Christian, reader. Are some of them religious at all? Let me say at once that, by sticking somewhat loosely to orthodoxy, I have attempted to broaden the meaning of the term "religious" to accommodate twentieth-century sensibility. And yet the interesting question arises as to how much good poetry could have been assembled, had one been confined to more orthodox and conventionally religious poems. During the last war, which were the true war poems? The ones that used "gimmicks" like Tobruk and flak, or the ones that conveyed the true and full experience of being at war? So with religion, it is not necessarily the poems couched in conventionally religious language that convey the truest religious experience.

The sections entitled 'God' and 'All' are comparatively straightforward. Under the first heading I have included poems that apostrophize God, such as Herbert's 'The Flower', as well as those which refer to Him as one of the Persons of the Holy Trinity. Under the heading 'All' will be found mostly poems which suggest a final position, whether it be of the soul, as in the short poem by Sir John Davies, or of the mind, as in some of the selections from Browning. The sections entitled 'It', 'Nothing', and 'Self' may be more controversial. There may be charges of humanism and pantheism. Earlier on, I referred to religion as the total response of the whole man, and later suggested that modern sensibility might wish to include more under the title 'Religious' than traditionalists could accept. That is why I have included under the heading 'Self' such a poem as Dylan Thomas's 'Fern Hill'. Is there much essential difference between this and a poem such as Vaughan's 'The Retreat'? Are we not coming to accept that, wherever and whenever man broods upon himself and his destiny, he does it as a spiritual and selfconscious being without peer in the universe which we know? It is for reasons like this that poets such as Edwin Muir and Miss Kathleen Raine are generously represented here.

In any discussion of religion and poetry, especially of orthodox religion, the question of symbol arises. The poet is assumed to speak with his own voice; the symbol is considered to have a somewhat overpowering or enervating effect. Hence, poets at the height of their powers might be expected to abjure symbols, being content to fall back on them only when their own powers had declined or were in abeyance. Wordsworth is a case in point. At the height of his powers he largely dispensed with Christian symbols; later, as his muse deserted him, he came to rely on them, or be satisfied with them, more and more. So the story goes. It is a short step from there to the equation of all the best poetry with the world, the flesh and the devil, and the second best with goodness and God. Blake put it most forcibly in his judgement of Milton. "He was a true poet," he said, "and of the devil's party without knowing it." It is not because I hold this view that I have included some of the poems to be found under the heading 'Nothing'. Neither the Middle Ages' obsession with death, nor the ability of contemporary poets such as John Crowe Ransom to describe despair so movingly, are necessarily indicative of their satanic allegiance. Poems such as the "terrible" sonnets of Gerard Manley Hopkins are but a human repetition of the cry from the Cross: "Eloi, Eloi, lama sabachthani!" The ability to be in hell is a spiritual prerogative, and proclaims the true nature of such a being. Without darkness, in the world we know, the light would go unprized; without evil, goodness would have no meaning. Over every poet's door is nailed Keats's saying about negative capability. Poetry is born of the tensions set up by the poet's ability to be "in uncertainties, mysteries, doubts, without any irritable reaching after fact and reason". Without the section entitled 'Nothing' I feel that the contents of this anthology would have been incomplete and its poetry the poorer.

Words and the Poet

(University of Wales Press: Cardiff, 1964), pp. 5-25

Words and the Poet[1]

There are personal reasons for my phrasing the title of this lecture thus. 'Language and Poetry' would be more abstract and would place too great a strain on my puny learning. Even 'Language and the Poet' would be beyond me, because the comparatively new subjects of linguistics and semantics are growing daily, and there is already a formidable bibliography of which I am almost entirely ignorant. I must fall back, therefore, on the components of language; not because of any specialised knowledge of them, but because they are the material which a poet uses. In so far as I have any claim to have written poems at all, it was with words that I made them; and I realise that, at the risk of wearying you, it must be about my concern with words that I must speak. But first of all, let us look as objectively as possible at words themselves; secondly at their usage by certain poets of the English tradition, and then finally at my own reactions to them, or treatment of them.

In considering words the first thing to remember is that they are the basic elements of speech. The basic utterance of a human being is a sound or a cry. But that is not strictly speaking, language, because sound in itself is barely significant; that is, it is not a sign of something else in the same way that a word is. The importance of a word is that with it we are able to make meaningful statements about objects which are not necessarily present. It is in this way that words lead to conceptual thought, which itself is the mark of a high degree of civilization.

I am already realising that the more one goes into the matter of words, the more difficult it becomes to treat them in isolation from language. But for reasons already given, I must do my best to avoid straying into the highly technical and controversial field of language itself. If there are any linguisticians present, I must ask them to excuse my naive and ignorant reflections on a subject which will be more familiar and no doubt more clear to themselves. For instance, it is always tempting to treat words rather like pebbles picked up on the beach; to turn them round, admiring their shape and texture, and to wonder how they came to be as they are. Why is a cat called so? This, of course, leads to etymology, and an extremely interesting discipline it is to trace the derivation of a word from its original existence in the parent language. In my small researches, however, I am not sure that I have been fortunate enough to drop on a satisfactory explanation as to how or why a certain word became applicable to a certain creature or object. Although they are so much later in time, one sometimes feels that the origins of a word are as mysterious as those of life itself. By what secret process did the name for a thing grow? Who first called it so? The question seems as insoluble as that which would ascertain the identity of the first man to strike sparks from a flint. Most of us know about the philosophical problems of nominalism and universals. Is there such a thing as beauty, or are there only beautiful things? Is it possible to think without language? Have you tried looking at a tree, a flower or a bird without its name echoing somewhere within you? To recognise something is to pull on the rope which makes its name ring. There is the primitive belief that the knowledge of a man's name gave one power over him. The young man who has seen a pretty girl will not rest until he has discovered her name.

I asked that we might look as objectively as possible at words. Is it possible? Does a word exist in its own right, or has it always a significatory function? The former possibility has excited many writers, notably Lewis Carroll. His 'Jabberwocky' has intrigued contemporary thinkers, because of the problem of literary reality. The "slithy toves" and the "borogoves" have no existence in our world of every day fact. They have no reference to empirically recognizable creatures or objects. Yet the imagination is capable of accepting them and apprehending them, even if through the medium of more ordered and rational concepts. The "toves" and the "borogoves" have a strange life of their own, and seem to raise almost insoluble problems. These problems recall, though they are not akin to, those raised by the standing of, say, Hamlet and King Lear. Hamlet and Lear never actually existed; Henry VIII and Sir

Philip Sidney did. How do we distinguish now between their position in the mind? Perhaps all one can say is something like this: The attempt to make words stand in their own right will have a limited reference, tend to be idiosyncratic or personal rather than universal. Fascinating as it is, Jaberwocky can never have more than the minor appeal of the grotesque, as compared with say, the controlled overtones of Shakespeare's verse. But to go into the problems arising out of the existence of Hamlet and Sir Philip Sidney would take us too far away from this matter of words to which I now return.

Whatever the doubts and problems arising over the actual being of words there is more general agreement about their personality, their accidents. Words are made up of consonants, vowels and syllables, accented and un-accented. These in their turn give rise to texture, pitch and rhythm. That is, there are long words and short words, soft and shrill, sharp and blunt; these characteristics often having little to do with the actual number of letters in the word. Miss Edith Sitwell has written much on this aspect of words, and it is the pre-occupation, conscious or unconscious of most poets. It is to Miss Sitwell that we are indebted for the comparison of vowels to the spirit, and consonants to the physical identity. That is, the consonants clothe the vowels finely or coarsely, and the vowels animate the word, gaily or gravely as the case may be. The consonants arrest or accelerate the movement of a line; the vowels provide the emotional overtones. Words have been likened to the bricks which go to build a sentence. So can they be likened to notes which build the poetic score. Sound is not the only, or even the most important aspect of English poetry, and the meaning of words must always be respected. Nevertheless the importance of the words in creating the music of a poem is obvious. I will have more to say about this aspect of words, when I come to particular poets' usage of words. But since we are trying in this first section to look at words as objectively and impersonally as possible, it might be interesting to look at some of the devices which are used by most poets at some time or other in the practice of their trade.

One of the first things that comes to mind is rhyme. We have, I suppose, at last shaken ourselves free of the idea that rhyme is essential to poetry. Still, it is often of considerable help, and need not be an end-line rhyme at all. In fact internal rhyme often has a much more subtle and moving effect. Then, too, there is the delayed

rhyme. I think it was A.E. who used to say that one should be led to
a rhyme as to the scent of a violet in a wood. Certainly there is a
peculiar charm in the echo of a delayed rhyme, as it comes back
from a word occurring perhaps several lines later than the original
word. What is the reason for the appeal of rhyme to the human ear?
Edward Sapir suggests that there is an underlying feeling in the
human being for what is right as regards tone and pronunciation. Is
it the sign of an ordered world of pattern into which things fit as
inevitably and satisfactorily as the pieces of a jig-saw puzzle? Is it the
human fondness for repetition? Certainly the English language is
rich in rhyme; not only in single, but in double rhyme. But further,
it is, of course, possible to produce triple and quadruple rhymes,
these in their turn being more suited to some purposes than to
others. For instance, single rhymes can have the necessary dignity
and gravity for great verse, or the pithiness of epigrammatic verse.
Double rhyme can introduce a sweet or pathetic element; but triple
and quadruple rhymes are confined almost entirely to light or
satirical verse, as in some of the delicious rhymes of Byron's 'Don
Juan'. But this is not to exhaust the possibilities of rhyme. There are
also half-rhymes, the assonantal and dissonantal rhyme scheme,
which have become popular with certain contemporary poets, partly
in an attempt to get away from the outworn traditional rhymes, and
partly to avoid the obviousness or the cloying effect of the full rhyme.
Wilfred Owen experimented with falling rhyme in order to convey
something of the tragedy and hopelessness of the first world war.
And certainly in a poem such as 'Strange Meeting' the continued
drop from one end word to another of lower pitch has a peculiarly
moving and mournful effect. With regard to other dissonantal
rhymes such as for instance "century" and "story", I am not sure
how much the effectiveness of this is not confined to the printed
word, tending to be lost or overlooked when recited orally. In this
connection, too, it is worth noting the contemporary fashion of
rhyming only the last syllable of a word, which enables words like
"wanted" to rhyme with "said" or "predicament" with "sent".
This can even be attenuated to the point where only the last letter is
made to rhyme; but here again this practice is somewhat recherché
and more apparent to the eye on the page than to the ear. However,
all these fashions are examples of the extraordinary flexibility and
potential of the word itself, and help to explain its fascination for the
practitioner.

But enough of rhyme. There are other things one can do with words. I have spoken of their texture. Obviously texture can be made to match the subject matter, or the subject matter can arise organically out of the poet's feeling for texture. In dramatic verse, for instance, at a particularly tense moment, the words will be of a staccato and breathless nature. When a sense of evil and menace is being conveyed, the texture of the words will be thick or oily. A certain roughness or strength in a character or scene will be expressed through a corresponding harshness of texture and so on. Some people find all this rather tedious and even far-fetched. Are we to suppose, they ask, that a poet does all this deliberately and consciously? Not exactly, of course. There is a large element of instinct about it. *Poeta nascitur non fit.* Yet years of learning and practising the art of poetry develop a poet's instinctive feeling for the right words and their manipulation. But there is a very conscious element present as well. In the act of composition every critical faculty of the poet is at work, choosing, refining, rejecting. *Le mot juste*! How much of the poet's time is taken up, not in searching for a rhyme, as used popularly to be supposed, but in seeking the right, the best, the most characteristic word, noun or adjective, as the case may be. There is little choice with pronouns and prepositions; it is with nouns and adjectives that a poet must work. Yeats said that a line might take hours to get right, but if it did not appear the work of a moment, all the labour was of no avail. It is worth remembering, when we read a poem and take for granted the felicitous phrasing, the happy choice of word or rhyme, that the so-called inspiration which produced it, was often as much due to the many hours of hard work and thought, as it was to instinct. As has been said already, and as Mallarmé stressed in his well-known remark, words are the poet's material; it is with words that poems are made. It is hard to think of any poet who has revolutionised or modified the English poetic tradition, whose main concern was not with language, and so basically with words. Each generation brings with it its own style, its own concern, its own discoveries. These must be discussed and disseminated among other ways through language. New terms, new connotations of words must be employed. The new wine cannot be put into the old bottles. And so each generation of poets is preoccupied with the problem of what language to use, of what words are suitable for poetry and what not. Sometimes there is a reversion to an earlier fashion; sometimes an almost complete break with tradition. English is made up roughly of two elements, the Anglo-Saxon and the Graeco-Roman. It is not all short or four-letter words that are Anglo-Saxon; not all compound or abstract ones that are Greek or Latin derivatives. Yet it might not be too misguided to take this as a rough generalisation. So with this in mind, the kind of words that would be most in favour could, to some extent, be inferred from the taste and preoccupations of the contemporary generation. Not that poets merely reflect those preoccupations. Being themselves the growing point of consciousness of a civilisation, it is often they who initiate. But not always. In his introduction to the *Faber Book of Modern Verse*, Michael Roberts referred to two kinds of poets, whom he classified roughly as European and English. The European kind of poet is more concerned with the defence of existing cultural values and has a wide reference; the poet in whom the English element predominates is more concerned with the poetic possibilities of the language. But this in itself is not a rigid division. Many good poets have had something of both in them. My main object is to stress the proper concern of a very large number of poets with language, and their achievements in building up out of its basic elements, words, poems which sometimes innovate, sometimes are traditional, but which always, in so far as they are good poems, bear the distinguishing mark of the craftsman with words who made them. And this brings me to my second point.

We have tried to think of words in general terms. We must now take more particular examples of their use by certain poets. Of course, the achievements of poets do not depend on their use of language alone. There is that peculiar rhythm and tone, which immediately distinguish certain poets; that indefinable style which belongs to others. There is their peculiar mastery of certain verse forms, to which no other poet has attained in the same measure; the stanzaic patterns which in some cases they initiated or made their own. But this is not my business at present. What of the words that they themselves use? There are certain things to be taken into consideration. There are the historical and geographical situations for instance. Few poets have survived from the more distant past; fewer still in popular esteem. Certain of their words, which would have been common enough to their contemporaries, have for us the flavour and consequent charm of their period. Chaucer comes immediately to mind. His earls and his knaves, so lusty and merry; his flowers that are fresh, and his fowls that sing sweetly, are for us now stamped with his name. There is Spenser, too, with his "rathe" primrose, and Skelton with his "blinkard blowbowl." Later comes Donne with the new words of his time such as cosmographer and optics. All these have the power to move us because of our position in the time scale relative to them. There is also a geographical or regional element bound up with words that are remote from us not in time but in space. The *locus classicus* is the Scottish border; but to a lesser extent there are dialect words on the Welsh border and in other regions of England, which can have a particularly moving effect. I served my curacy in an area where people who were sensitive to the cold were "nesh." My first living was in a district that was "sniving" with rabbits; where the dead grass was known as "feg" and the manure heap as the "mixen". In Ireland, as writers such as Synge found, they cut turf not peat, and people are destroyed by pain. To what extent great verse can incorporate such dialect elements is a problem. Williams Barnes was obsessed by it; Tennyson to a less extent. Hardy and Lawrence both gave it some attention. It is more adaptable by the novelist, because in dialogue it can convey both character and class. In poetry it mostly requires footnotes, which militate against the enjoyment of the verse. But perhaps I have said enough in this connection to indicate that the charm arising from such words is not of the essence of poetry. There are, of course, certain words which are seminal in different cultural epochs, and insofar as a poet is capable of embracing most aspects of current knowledge, these words will be found in his verse. But the very character and interests of the poet will lead him to pay more attention to some than to others. "Webster was much possessed by death," wrote Mr. Eliot, and that would be true of the majority of the Elizabethans, I suppose. Consequently words like "blood" and "bone" and "dark" tend to recur in their work. I have not the learning behind me to quote at any length, but I imagine that fairly close attention to a number of poets would, from the recurrence of certain words, be revelatory of their chief concerns and obsessions, as well as the sort of persons they were. Is it illegitimate to attribute to Chaucer a certain vigour of temperament, a capacity for delight in the natural world and in all mankind? His verse is full of words like "lusty" and "merry," "fresh" and "fair," "pleasaunce" and "jolitee". I realize that this suggestion must not be pressed too far, remembering Yeats' theory of the masks, and also that the poetic persona can be compensatory. Tough men do not necessarily write

tough verse; nor gentle men gentle verse. Even Yeats marvelled that
a man of such gentle manners as Synge could arouse such wild and
unruly passions in his audiences. But Synge had already said that
verse had become mawkish and before it could become human
again, would have to learn to grow brutal.

Still, all that by the way. I must adhere to my belief that there is
probably something symptomatic in words that tend to recur in a
poet's work. Vaughan was continually moved by such concepts as
light. Swinburne loved the sea, Shelley the air, and so on. But all
this suggests that I am thinking primarily of nouns, which is a little
obvious. It has been said that the true test of a poet is to be seen in
his use of adjectives. I agree. But not only are adjectives the criterion
of a poet, they are also much more subtly revelatory. Apart from
dramatic verse, where the poet is portraying differing characters, is
it not probable that, very often unconsciously, the poet will describe
or choose for his attention objects and people, who possess the
accidents that appeal to or fascinate him? There is a wide field here
for reading and study. Once we get away from the conventions of
earlier verse, we must begin to look at the more individual treatment
of adjectives; and from what I have implied by the word convention,
we should expect adjectives to play an increasingly important role in
contemporary verse. Let us look for a moment at a few poets in their
use of adjectives and epithets.

> Is this the face that launched a thousand ships
> And burnt the topless towers of Ilium?

I like "topless". Of course, it alliterates with "towers" and echoes
the "p" in "ships". But there is more to it than that. It has
abundance. I like, too, Skelton's Elinor Rumming, who was all
"foggy fat". I am not sure how far to take the word at face value,
but if I can, then it has been echoed by Miss Marianne Moore's
"elephants with their fog coloured skin". But Skelton's adjective is
the more brilliant. It suggests texture as well as colour; and smell,
too, if you like! I don't know if it was Shakespeare who wrote of the
robin: "That hath the ruddy breast and bugle eyes, and is the yellow
autumn's nightingale". But "bugle" has all the genius we expect of
Shakespeare, and notice how "yellow" is so faintly and beautifully
echoed by "gale". Shakespeare is, of course, full of these apt and
striking adjectives, could we but call them to mind. Remember the
lion in *Julius Caesar* that "glared upon him and went surly by".

Then there is the "rooky" wood in *Macbeth*. There is Hamlet's "majestical roof fretted with golden fire". Notice the "fretted". And what about Cleopatra's scene with its "curled Anthony" and "downy windows", both marvels of evocation. Remember, too, the hounds in *A Mid-Summer Night's Dream* "so flewed, so sanded". But after all Shakespeare is a mine, where we could dig for days, and we must move on; move on quite a bit, stopping only to glance at the adjective "natural" in *Paradise Lost*. "Some natural tears they dropped, but wiped them soon". That word "natural" is very expressive of the times in which Milton lived, and informs us fairly clearly both of Milton's character and of his theology. I can think of no striking adjectives after this until we come to the Romantics. There is not a great deal in Wordsworth, although I like the lines on Chatterton: "The sleepless soul that perished in his pride". One must always remember, too, that it was Wordsworth who helped Coleridge out with one of his stanzas in 'The Ancient Mariner'.

> I fear thee, ancient mariner,
> I fear thy skinny hand...

Coleridge began, and Wordsworth added:

> And thou art long, and lank, and brown,
> As is the ribbed sea-sand.

If "lank" is good, "ribbed" is brilliant. I don't feel that Shelley is the place to look for original adjectives, but I have always liked his "melancholy thunder" in 'Adonais'. And Keats, what of him? There are many examples here: "The moving waters at their priestly task"; "the wailful choir of gnats"; the "perilous seas"; and the lover's "peerless eyes". And Keats himself draws attention to the power of adjectives in his ruminations on the word "forlorn": "the very word is like a bell to toll me back from thee to my sole self". These are all clear and very familiar. So are some of Tennyson's: "the gray-eyed morn"; "the lusty trout"; "the bearded meteor" and "the brimming river". Indeed, they are so familiar, so part of English literature, that we do not always remember to give sufficient credit to the master who first thought of them. But I am tiring you. We have dallied long enough with the great masters. I will close this discussion of adjectives by drawing attention to some examples from contemporary poets. What one notices in them, I think, is a tendency to put more of the poem's weight on the adjectives. Poems tend to be more contrived to-day. We know more about poetry and are sometimes very brilliant in achieving effects, but there is often enough little else there. The older poets took these things in their stride; we pride ourselves on a rather common-place poem, if it has one or two unusual adjectives in it. Still, we must give credit where credit is due. The effects are there, and very enjoyable and enlightening they can be. I will begin with Yeats. Every autumn, as I see the birches turn golden, I think of his "leopard-coloured trees". That was at the beginning of his career. At his maturity comes the richer and more profound adjective "resinous"—"man's own resinous heart". It forms an interesting test in practical criticism, does it not? If asked who, out of the whole range of English poetry, was the author of that phrase, would not W.B.Yeats occur to one as a first guess?

One of the aims of the Imagists, as expressed in their manifesto of 1913, was to use always the exact word. Consequently, we might expect quite a few trenchant and pithy adjectives from a study of their work. But I am not sure how much we shall find outside the poetry of Marianne Moore. Miss Moore is a scrupulous craftswoman. For her, swans have "gondoliering legs", and snakes "hypodermic teeth". Linnets are "spinet sweet" and jelly-fish "ink be-spattered". But strongly idiosyncratic poets are not going to be bound by the supposed need for the exact word. They give their own descriptions of things and people, making us see them as they saw them. The example that comes most readily to mind is Dylan Thomas. Some of his adjectives merely exemplify Pope's line: "What oft was thought, but ne'er so well expressed". I am thinking of those such as the "lunar silences" and the "golden weather". But when we come to phrases such as "sour humble hands", "dung-hills, white as wool", and especially "whinnying green stable", we have examples of that peculiar talent, which helped to make Dylan Thomas, at his best, so fascinating. It was also a talent which was sure to evoke a good deal of unsuccessful imitation in lesser poets, who illustrate the difference between a truly idiosyncratic writer, doing what he does because it is right for him to do it, and those who do it, or try to, because it is clever or fashionable. An interesting exception to this is W.S.Graham, who, beginning as I opined, very much under the influence of Dylan Thomas, quickly developed his own individual style and language. Most, if not all, of the poems in his second book, *The Night Fishing*, are about the sea. Consequently his adjectives are such as to evoke the things and the atmosphere of the sea, and the west coast of Scotland, which are his themes. He writes of the "sheared water", "the scaling light", "the mewing firth" and such like. He is interesting, too, for his ability to turn a conventional phrase to his use. I dare say you are familiar with the conventional terms for numbers of birds, such as a wisp of snipe, a charm of goldfinches, and a spring of teal. Well Graham turns the last to his use by referring quite naturally, but very originally to the "springing teal". However, it is not altogether legitimate for me to quote Graham as an exponent of the use of adjectives, because his is an active, muscular verse, and its real individuality is more apparent in the verbs. From which you may conclude that I consider adjectives to be the mark of the poet as observer, and verbs of the poet as participator. And that is as likely a theory as any.

This matter of adjectives is far from exhausted, but I don't expect you are, so we had better move on, glancing merely at one lovely example by Edwin Muir. In one of his poems, he refers to Plato in his "radiant world". Equating, as we do, Greece with the dawn of civilization in Europe, we can see the peculiar aptness and beauty of this adjective that qualifies the world of the Athenian thinker.

For the last few minutes or so, I have chosen to dwell on the function of nouns, and more especially adjectives, in the creation of poetry, and that function is a very real and prominent one. But even in doing so, I realize that I am open to the charge of murdering to dissect. One can't really take poetry to pieces like this. A poem is an organic whole, and more than the sum of its parts. The same difficulty is experienced in paying too much attention to content at the expense of sound and vice versa. The sound of a poem is part of its meaning; so are the nouns and adjectives; and like the organs of a living body, they become lifeless when cut off from that body. Even short, one-syllable pronouns and prepositions have their part to play. Consider a simple phrase like "go for". The dog will go for you. So, using Ruskin's pathetic fallacy, we could write: "It was a wild day; the wind went for the trees". It is after all so often the phrase, the metaphor, that is the kernel of poetry. But even in admitting this, we must allow that phrases and metaphors are but words in conjunction or counterpoint. The mention of metaphor tempts me to turn aside once more to consider that high degree of sophistication and mastery of a language, which enables one to play on words. One thinks immediately of Yeats' "Mrs. French, gifted with so fine an ear''. But I really feel that I must proceed without further delay to my third point, which was, you may remember, my own attitude to words, what they mean to me, and how I try to use them.

I realize only too well that it is not for any scholarly attainments of any specialised knowledge of the subject that I have been asked to give this lecture, but simply because of the fact that I myself write what passes for poetry, and am, therefore, a practitioner with words. And although, in virtue of this, most poets should have a common approach to words, there are bound to be certain individual differences. Some poets, as I have already suggested, will have a leaning towards certain words rather than others. One poet will be preoccupied with a different problem from another, and will be using words in a different way or for a different purpose. I think you may find that, in this final section, I ask more questions than I answer, but perhaps that is inevitable when dealing with one's own personal approach to anything as intransigent as words.

One of the first questions that arises for a Welshman face to face with the English tongue is: What is my true feeling for these words? Am I fascinated, repelled, resentful? A case used to be made out for the debt contemporary English literature owed to the Celtic fringe. English writing, it was said, had reached such a state of debility, that it could only be revived by frequent transfusions of Celtic blood. Expatriate Scots, Irish and Welsh, coming as many of them did, from vernacular areas, were the very men to put new vigour into the worn out veins of English. As proof there were Yeats, Synge and Joyce from Ireland, and Dylan Thomas from Wales, to name only a few. Whatever the merits of this argument, I think we will find that the manner in which the contribution is made will vary according to the writer's attitude to his medium. Where he is a willing exile, associating his native speech and locality with a backward stage in man's progress towards the English millenium, he will delight in the newly-discovered riches of English words. Where he has a real love and respect for his native traditions, he will regret his enforced separation from them and resent the necessity of having to use words, which to all intents and purposes are those of a foreign people. One of the problems of an Anglo-Welsh poet in any part of Welsh-speaking Wales is that of having to try to transpose the raw material of his imagination and experience into the alien medium of English speech which has no exact equivalents for *mynydd* and *bwlch*, *cwm* and *hafod*; poetry being, as all will allow, in the last resort untranslatable.

I mention that as personally applicable. But I am not unaware of the possible fascination of the opposite, the different, the alien. Welsh speakers display this in their conversation, their preaching. How often one has heard a Welsh preacher mention some phrase such as *cariad Duw* and then shout all over the chapel "the love of God" as though that were a much more effective way of driving it home! Or in conversation a speaker will say, referring to some enthusiast: *O, y mae ganddo* "interest" *yn y peth*, as though interest were infinitely more expressive, and more respectable than *diddordeb*. But there can be none of this macaronic nonsense in the writing of English poetry, *pace* Ezra Pound, and to a lesser extent T.S.Eliot. One must take the words as one finds them, and make them sing. And here arises another question: Are words the poet's servant or master? We are familiar, no doubt, with Mr.Eliot's pessimistic conclusions in 'East Coker' although he wins through to some sort of détente in 'Little Gidding', where he speaks of "the complete consort dancing together". I think that any practising poet would agree that there can be no hard and fast rule in this matter. Most poets compose with great difficulty, choosing and rejecting and altering their words, until often the finished draft bears little relation to what they began with. In this way, the poet would seem to be the master, forcing the words to do the bidding of the conscious mind. Yet this, also, is a travesty of the position. Words have surprising resilience, and get their own way often by appearing to yield. The idea of the poet's eye "in a fine frenzy rolling" and of the words flowing ready mixed with the ink of the tip of his pen is, of course, a fiction. Yet here again most poets could tell of periods of inspiration of varying length, when the words and lines did appear to come with agreeable ease. And although we have Yeats' words as a warning against being deceived by an appearance of ease, we also have it on Mr.Vernon Watkins' authority that he said, too, that a poem is a piece of luck. This is a pregnant statement, but certainly one aspect of it has to do with words themselves—a lucky finding or perception of the right word, the felicitous phrase or brilliant metaphor. Is it not to this luck that we owe so many of the adjectives to which I have referred? I don't want to detract from the poet's art at all; but perhaps we understand a little better in these days of extra-sensory perception the true nature of magic and luck. Assuredly I should consider myself lucky rather than clever to have hit on a word like "resinous" as an adjective qualifying the human heart; and yet I probably never would have happened on it, not only because I am not W.B.Yeats, and am without his talent, but also because my aims and way of looking at life, the whole organization of my personality are different, not to mention inferior. At least one would like to think that the least any competent poet can do is to put words in their place, which was one of Coleridge's definitions of poetry—"the best words in the best order". But even if we can agree as to the best words, what is the best order? Some poets have found it necessary to distort the syntax of their poems in accordance with their own peculiarly violent or tragic or individual view of life, as for instance Gerard Manley Hopkins and e.e.cummings.

Is there a way through this jungle? Can one make any useful generalisations? It seems that it has always been easier for poets to evolve theories of language than to stick to them. Wordsworth was a case in point; Yeats another. It was Coleridge who remarked that the lofty and sustained diction which characterised Wordsworth as a poet was a complete contradiction of his theory about the speech of natural man. And although Yeats had a temporary spasm for deleting from his verse all words which were not understood by Irish washerwomen, fortunately for the state of English poetry the lunacy passed. I would be inclined to doubt whether much poetry of top rank has ever been written in accordance with a theory. Wordsworth at his most puling lends me support. It is better far to observe, not necessarily consciously, what you are able to do with words, and what they can do to you, and on that basis, *post hoc*, as it were, to evolve your theory of poetry. Personally I have often agreed that there is something feminine about words, and, of course, the muse herself is female. It is as though the more one woos words, the more desperately in love with them one grows, the more coquettish and refractory they become; whereas a certain insouciance or aloofness in the writer will often bring them fawning about his feet. But I realise that such an attitude is based more on the craftsman's, the maker's approach to poetry. This is what is sometimes rather contemptuously referred to as pure poetry. A pure poet is one who, presumably, lives for his art, interested in the interior world of words and thought, rather than in the everyday world of noise and pain and evil. I think, when I examine my own position, that I have never been a pure poet in that way. To make a poetic artefact out of

words has never, or rarely ever been my first aim or satisfaction.
There is always lurking in the back of my poetry a kind of moralistic
or propogandist intention. It is as though, having found that I had a
slight gift for putting words together to make poems, I used that gift
as the best way I knew for getting a particular message across. The
two things that appeal most strongly to my imagination are Wales
and nature, especially as the latter manifests itself as the background
to a way of life. I believe that there is profound and lasting value in
both concepts. Consequently I am tempted to preach this sermon in
verse. This leads to the employment of special words, nouns drawn
from the natural background and adjectives descriptive of it. I shall
have a little more to add to this before concluding. Coomaraswamy
said that an artist is not a special kind of man, but that every man is
a special kind of artist. This seems to be one of those rather slick
half-truths which so often gain currency. Indeed, no one wishes to
set up artists as a kind of *herren-volk*. The difference between them
and other men is quite possibly a difference in degree and not in
kind. But the degree is very great in the best of them. I suppose most
men wish to tell others of their experiences. They gratify this wish
mainly in talk, that endless noise which goes on in streets and 'buses
and pubs. But some few have been born with the urge and the gift to
write about their experiences, many in prose, fewer in poetry. I am
using experience in a very broad sense to embrace every
apprehension of life by the total personality. In other words, as I go
through my day at my desk, in my contact with others, or out in the
world of nature, I see something, begin to turn it over in my mind,
and decide that it has poetic possibilities. The main concern now will
be not to kill it; not to make it common, prosaic, uninteresting. If it
bores me in the telling, it will surely bore the public in the reading. I
must choose words and rhythms which will keep it fresh and have
the power to recreate the experience in all its original intensity for
each new reader. But in this very process the experience is changed,
and will continue to be changed as each new reader apprehends it.

A recurring ideal, I find, is that of simplicity. At times there comes
the desire to write with great precision and clarity, words so simple
and moving that they bring tears to the eyes, or, if you like, as
Wordsworth said, are "too deep for tears". This is not peculiar to
writers. Most people, when they are profoundly moved by sorrow or
anger, tend to pick their words carefully, so that they may have their
full impact. This is where the one syllable, the four letter words

come into their own. They can have particular force. One remembers lines such as that by Wilfred Owen in 'Futility': "Was it for this the clay grew tall?" Plain simple English words, yet so often they are the best. It is a case of "central peace subsisting at the heart of endless agitation". Art is not simple, and yet about so much of the best, whether in painting, poetry or music, there is a kind of miraculous simplicity. Some of Shakespeare's greatest effects are produced with everyday words. There is Lear's "Take it away; it smells of mortality"; or Cleopatra's "Do you not see my baby at my breast, that sucks the nurse asleep?" Then there are the ballads and the 'Ancient Mariner', and Blake. I think that as long as there is poetry, it will keep reverting to that native plainess and simplicity. There will be reactions and revolutions because of the common human need for variety and change; the pendulum will swing to and fro; but somewhere, not too far in the background, there will always be that basic simplicity. This, in a way, was the impetus behind Imagism. But there is a problem bound up with the question of the exact word. Significant poems seem not to be written about Stone Curlews, Dartford Warblers and Lesser Spotted Woodpeckers, nor about military orchids, water lobelia and antirrhinums, but rather about birds and flowers. We like to think of every poet as possessing a very keen eye, whereas Yeats, for instance, was reputed to be decidedly short-sighted. It is as though, for poetry, general words will do, with occasional glimpses or insights for added effect, as in Rosetti's "The woodspurge has a cup of three".

I said I would conclude with some more observations on words and the natural background. I live in the country by choice. The events of nature are very real to me. I am never far from agricultural activity, the traditional occupation of man. Once an eye for nature and a flair for describing it were the normal appurtenances of a poet. Even if the audience were townspeople, the fields were never far away, the towns being small. Most of that has changed and is going to change still more. The common environment of the majority is an urban-industrial one. The potential audience of a poet is one of town dwellers, who are mostly out of touch, if not out of sympathy with nature. Their contact with it is modified by the machine. This is tending to deprive country-rooted words of their relevance. The new modes of experience, the new subjects, the new vocabulary are creating the impression that the old words are outmoded. Rossetti's word-spurge has given way to "the belt feed lever and the belt holding pawl'' of Richard Eberhart. And this is a problem which all poets must face. I don't allow for a moment the superiority of urban to country life. I don't believe that town life is any more real than rural. I don't believe that a poet who chooses to write about an agricultural environment is necessarily insular, escapist or even provincial. But the fact remains that a very different kind of life is being lived by a majority of the people in this country now, and that most of the everyday objects of their world have new, often technical names. A vast amount of new knowledge is accumulating, with its accompanying vocabulary. One of the great questions facing the poet is: Can significant poetry be made with these new words and terms? In theory the answer is frequently an affirmative one. People say: ''I don't see why not''. They quote words such as chromosomes as being actually attractive. My own position is usually to allow this as a legitimate theory, but to ask in practice, ''Where are the poems?''

Perhaps it is my ignorance of other languages that makes me say this. Maybe they are issuing from the presses in Germany or Czecho-Slovakia. Maybe it is too soon, and there has not yet been time to assimilate or absorb the enormous amount of fresh knowledge and its vocabulary. But I remember Coleridge's saying to the effect that the opposite of poetry is not prose but science. We have yet to prove that we can have both. I remember also Wordsworth's ''human heart by which we live.'' The poet's function and privilege surely is to speak to our condition in the name of our common humanity in words which do not grow old because the heart does not grow old.

Note
1. This is the text of the W.D.Thomas Memorial Lecture that R.S. Thomas delivered at the University College of Swansea in November 1963.

A Frame for Poetry

TLS, 3 March 1966, p. 169

A Frame for Poetry

"When I mention religion, I mean the Christian religion; and not only the Christian religion but the Protestant religion; and not only the Protestant religion but the Church of England." So the Reverend Mr. Thwackum; just as simple as that. But as we smile we disguise the need for definition. How shall we define such enormous subjects, or discover definitions that are generally acceptable? Men have been trying to define poetry for centuries and have hardly progressed much further than "the stuff that poets write". But on that level, what is religion? The trouble is that so many of those who find connexions between poetry and religion do so by *petitio principii*. Still, one must take that risk

As far as religion is concerned, Thwackum was too narrow or too cavalier. But was he altogether on the wrong track? He lived as we do in the western world. Our language, like his, is English, our religious inheritance Christian. Can we have a workable definition of religion for a twentieth-century Englishman that is not in some way Christian? Or must we be eclectic or syncretist, and out of the bits and pieces of our global consciousness fashion a new religious mosaic, brilliant but bewildering? It may have a steadying effect on our discussion if we confine ourselves to the Christian presentation of religious experience. But it will be far from solving all our problems.

If we agree that for most English people religion equals Christianity, there is still the task of defining the latter. The modern obsession with primitive Christianity suggests that the faith has not remained untouched by the centuries. And why should it? Still the problem remains. What is Christianity? Christ or the Church? Or both? The Trinitarian formula is wide enough, and unassailable by modern psychology, but not all Christian dogma is so. And yet those who grow bitter about the Church forget the cathedrals, the paintings, the sculpture, the scriptures themselves, as well as the lives of those of her members who have been inspired by Bible and Prayer Book and sustained by the Sacrament.

The point is that it is within the scope of poetry to express or convey religious truth, and to do so in a more intense and memorable way than any other literary form is able to. Religion has to do first of all with vision, revelation, and these are best told of in poetry. The interesting feature though of a missionary religion such as Christianity is the way it maintains a reciprocal relationship with the culture of its converts. The main reason for this surely is the poetic nature of the original message, which allows itself to be interpreted and expressed in an infinite number of new ways. ''Jesus Christ the same yesterday, today and for ever'', is assuredly one of the hard sayings of the Bible. If the message is the man, then Jesus was a poet, and he changes and grows as each new epoch explores and develops the resources of that living poetry.

In another sense, he is God's metaphor, and speaks to us so. ''He that hath seen me hath seen the Father.'' ''I am the bread of life.'' ''And I, if I be lifted up, will draw all men unto me.'' How can anyone who is not a poet ever fully understand the gospels with their accumulation of metaphor? ''How can this man give us his flesh to eat?'' Yet, how shall we attempt to describe or express ultimate reality except through metaphor or symbol?

One gets the impression of a general dissatisfaction with Christianity as too rarefied, too mythical, too unrelated to the world of flesh and blood. Yet it has been well called the most material of the great religions. ''The Word was made flesh and dwelt among us.'' ''I believe in the resurrection of the body.'' Its concern with the minute particulars is obvious; in what other religion worthy of the name do flesh and blood, bread and wine, earth and water, beasts and flowers play so prominent and important a part? I do not wish to be too restrictive in my interpretation of Christianity. There are, I know, degrees of vision and experience within it, and these have to be acknowledged. Some of the chief mystics and saints have advanced far along the way to the Beatific Vision, where all sense imagery is transcended. What I am concerned with here is the relation of religion to poetry, which is something that is mediated to us via the symbol of language, "a local habitation and a name". Mr. Allen Tate has distinguished between what he calls the angelic imagination and the symbolic imagination, maintaining that the business of the poet is primarily with the latter. He quotes Charles Williams to show how even so supreme a poet as Dante invariably started from the common thing.

> I' fui nato e cresciuto
> sovra 'l bel fiume d'Arno all gran villa,
> e son col corpo ch' i' ho sempre avuto.[1]

The Divine Comedy is based on a homely foundation of common and palpable things, however high its uppermost towers soar. When we turn to the founder of Christianity, we find no essential difference. It was upon the simple things of life that Jesus based his message, the sower and the seed, the shepherd and his flock. When he wished to institute a service which could express and convey the essence of his teaching, he took bread and wine and consecrated them, metaphors of that love and sacrifice which are of the very essence of eternal life.

The story is similar throughout the history of English poetry. Admittedly there is a dew on much early English verse, attributable in part perhaps to the purity of medieval Christianity, and in part to the newness of the language itself. I am thinking especially of such miracles as 'I sing of a maiden', and 'Maid of the Mor'. In Chaucer and Spenser, in the Border Ballads and through Shakespeare down to Blake himself there is the same ability to elicit "thoughts that do often lie too deep for tears" from the common things of this mortal life.

> I canna look on that bonny face, where it lies in the grass.[2]

> Embrouded was he as it were a mede
> Al ful of fresshe floures, whyte and rede.[3]

> Ah, Sun-flower! weary of time
> Who countest the steps of the Sun:[4]

There are certain fundamental misunderstandings which may be endemic in our secular society. The two professions of priest and poet are so divorced in the public eye as to be quite beyond the possibility of symbiosis. I realize that there are certain precedents for this attitude. There are Arnold's approval of the reaction from the Puritan absorption, and the misgivings of Gerard Manley Hopkins.

There is also Blake's cryptic remark about Milton's being a true
poet and of the devil's party without knowing it. But leaving aside
such celebrated instances, let us admit a generally held opinion that
"poetry is not made by feeble blood", but has largely to do with the
world, the flesh and the devil; that Christian doctrine and discipline
exercise a restrictive, if not to say stifling, influence on poetry, and
that, therefore, the true poet cannot tolerate such bonds. And as a
corollary of this that a Christian, and more especially a parson, can
be expected to feel ill at ease in the presence of some of the rawer
facts of life. For instance, I myself have been criticized for including
in an anthology of religious verse a poem describing some of the
more biological functions of the human body. The poem was
adjudged obscene, and yet if the ordinary parts and functions of the
human body cannot be viewed as holy, what can? And what are we
to make of the Incarnation? It seems that we have come a long way
from the figure of Jesus of Nazareth, the friend of publicans and
sinners, "a man gluttonous and a wine-bibber", who said to the
whore, "neither do I condemn thee. Go, and sin no more"; who
ended his mortal life upon a cross in the midday heat of Palestine
with the blood dripping from the wounds of the nails. Allen Tate in
his essay called 'The Symbolic Imagination', from which I have
already quoted, has some pertinent things to say about "the great
fragrance of blood" which St. Catherine of Siena experienced.
"Only persons of extraordinary courage and perhaps genius even",
says Mr. Tate, "can face the spiritual truth in its physical body."

Perhaps the two most diagnostic features of our present age are its
secularism and its abstractionism; they exact their toll, both
spiritually and culturally. So far as we can tell, there are no works of
poetry being produced in English today that are of comparable
stature with those of Chaucer, Spenser, Shakespeare or Milton.
Whether these writers themselves were avowedly Christian or not,
they wrote within a Christian framework. Is there a relation between
the decline of Christianity in Britain and the decline in works of high
poetry? Many like to associate poetic decline or inferiority with a
consciously adopted Christianity, Wordsworth being the *locus
classicus*. But why blame Christianity for our failure to produce high
poetry, if Christianity is no longer a major force in our culture? It is
not really Christianity which is on trial but Christian dogma. It is
true that the natural tendency of all preserved revelation is to
crystallize and dessicate, but with a structure on the scale of the

Church, it is dangerous to generalize. There are Hymns Ancient and Modern but there are also the King James's Bible and the Book of Common Prayer. There are the vested interests, the failure of certain bishops and councils and theologians, but there are also the Herberts and Ferrars and an innumerable company of ordinary churchmen, who have refreshed themselves daily in the very doctrines and disciplines which are supposed by the critics to have such deadening effect.

Hardening of the arteries seems to be an occupational hazard for lyric poets, so that it would appear a trifle unfair to attach any blame to their professed religion. But there are other considerations. Admittedly there is the temptation to propagandize on behalf of one's beliefs, but this has to be resisted, just as the pressures of a secular age must be resisted. This latter, perhaps, is the more difficult, since not only will explicitly Christian poetry fall on deaf ears, but the implicitly Christian will be overlooked. In such circumstances it is difficult to decide whether a waning Christianity or a waxing secularism is the more to blame. However, perhaps one of the most damaging accusations that can be brought against secularism is its involvement with the commercial element, with the tendency to appraise art and letters in terms of their saleability. There is also the absurd arrogance of supposing that we now stand at the zenith of human history as the final judges, when actually we are the prisoners of an age which is at best unimaginative. One must not generalize too freely about science any more than about Christianity. It has many branches, some of them perhaps poetic in themselves. But in considering poetry and secularism, I asked whether there was a connexion between the decline of Christianity in Britain and the decline of works of high poetry. One might ask a similar question in relation to science?

We are told with increasing vehemence that this is a scientific age, and that science is transforming the world, but is it not also a mechanized and impersonal age, an analytic and clinical one; an age in which under the hard gloss of affluence there can be detected the murmuring of the starved heart and the uneasy spirit? "The voice of Rachel crying for her children, and would not be comforted, because they are not." The old themes of poetry are outmoded, we are told. Nothing is in itself un-poetical and true poets can as well make poetry about tractors and conveyor-belts as about skylarks and nightingales. In theory, yes, but in practice where is the poetry?

> I say the acknowledgement of God in Christ,
> Accepted by thy reason, solves for thee
> All questions in the earth and out of it.

Perhaps it is the attempt of contemporary Christianity to be reasonable in the face of science that makes it so innocuous. It is certainly our increasing isolation by science from Geoffrey Hill's "common, puddled substance" that makes us less and less capable of statements like "a deep distress hath humanised my soul", and so less and less capable of sustaining that creative tension of the intellect and the emotions out of which the good life and the good poem can be born.

Notes
1. From Dante's 'Inferno' (canto 23, lines 94-96): " 'I was born and grew up on the fair stream of Arno, in the great city, and with the body I have always had' ".
2. From a Scottish ballad entitled 'Edom o' Gordon'.
3. From Chaucer's description of the Squire in 'The Prologue' to *The Canterbury Tales*.
4. The opening lines of Blake's 'Ah! Sun-Flower'.

The Mountains

(Chilmark Press: New York, 1968), pp. 14-42

The Mountains

Some days you can't see them. The eye bumps into black cloud, low down. Nearer there is the sound of water, tumbling from wet heights. There is no light, no colour; only grey and green, and the wind blowing. A place to think of firelight in, and blankets and hot tea. And the small column picks its way earthward with its broken burden. He fell on the slippery rocks, and lay soaking and starving, while his companions went back down to the inn. A sheep's cry falls like a stone.

Further down the houses begin, the rows of drab dwellings; wrenched from the siopes, with wet roofs, permanently wet. Their plots marked off with slate fences. Places of spittle and cold phlegm. Women swab the steps that are never dry. Late, lonely buses climb up to them, a brief gaudiness in a vast gloom. These people know the mountains, but do not ascend them. They gnaw at them for small pay, and die early, silted up. The bare, hideous chapels ache for an hour with sad words and fierce singing; the futile memorials are planted in rows.

It is so often raining in the mountains; sometimes great rods of it, like the bars of a prison, though shining silver against the darkness of the far slope. But suddenly the sun is switched on, and the valley is full of golden leaves like a tree undressing. There are clear days, too; the cloud's masonry piled up untidily above the honeyed mountains, the long slopes bruised with shadow. From Conway the hills rise, become mountains, soaring shoulders above the narrowing valley. From Anglesey they are spread out in a long wave that threatens but never falls. Hundreds of windows reflect the sun as it goes down. Approaching from the sea, from Ireland, you see them towering,

smudging the horizon. Coming up England at dusk these are the
ramparts of old castles with the sky smoking, red. The passes are
deep, dark and entered in fear. In the old days you took the train,
got out in darkness at some lonely halt, and beyond the one lamp
with its guttering flame you saw the shapes loom and heard the
water being broken. Or you looked into a still lake and saw the
mountains meet on its surface; a thin stream of sky between, where
the stars floated.

Moonlight in the mountains! The traveller set out from the inn to
cross the pass, and heard the hoof-beats following up the long track.
Time has not erased the shadow of the rider from the hillside, nor
that of his huge horse. And when the wind is up and whinnying, the
clouds go galloping and the coach races. It is a country to be abroad
in; greetings in a strange tongue or sly smiles from over a hedge.
Mountain men are lean, bramble-sinewed, sharp-boned. The cliff's
curtain is drawn against them. It is so still at times; they can hear the
peregrine on the ledges chattering; *y gwalch glas*.[1] Then the ripping of
the air, as it stoops. A few indolent feathers silently descend. So the
Welsh chieftains struck their enemies in the old days. To one looking
up at the rock face streams pour out of the sky. Further up are the
amphitheatres; hidden audiences wait to be addressed. A raven flaps
across the area of blue sky, guttural, powerful, the wind whirring
through his black webs. Above the high pass is a stone, tall, slender.
It has deceived for centuries with its human likeness, poised
motionless above the road; arrested how many aeons ago on its
downward plunge. Time has worn against it. It is not eroded.
Lichens embroider it; polecats mate in its shadow. The buzzard
feathers its prey on its rough shoulders. It has a grudge against men.
One day some William Jones will pass that way in his new car. It
will fall and kill him.

It is the silence of the mountains. Far down on the main road the
cars crawl, but make no noise. There is a woolliness of the ears,
muffling the footsteps. One inhabits a monastry of glass. Some days
each blade of glass shines; some days there is mist in a hurry, endless
skeins untangling themselves. You look down through swirling
vapour, where wind grapples the cloud, and the heather twitches.
Loneliness comes, the fear of falling. Life looks into the eyes of
death, and time is enormous, unaware of the human.

This is to know a mountain; to inch one's way up it from ledge to
ledge; to break one's nails on its surface. To feel for handholds, for

footholds, face pressed to its stone cheek. The long look at the traverse, the scrutiny of each fissure. And the thought that it has all been done before is of no help. There is the huge tug of gravity, the desire of the bone for the ground, with the dogged spirit hauling the flesh upward. Rare flowers tremble, waver, just out of reach. From the summit the voices fall, a careless garland. A girl stands with her back to the drop. A slim figure, she leads the mountain by a rope. It will not try to master her again? The next time there will be snow, ice. The mountain will digest her slowly.

Each person brings his load to the top and sets it down. The cairns grow, monuments of an achieved hope. On good days you can see the sea with its yellow trimming of sand, and the land in between primitively folded. Or far away to the south there are more mountains with the desire to climb them; to be there rather than here. And the lakes! A hundred of them; blue windows ventilating the land. But no fish in them; no birds feeding at the brim. Barren and cold and deep: terrible wounds the water has filled but not healed.

On the warmest of days there is the shadow; places the sun never reaches. Coldness like a cloth flung in the face, and the slow tick of water. Delicate, flowerless plants, fringing the entrance to a hole, and the damp musty smell pinching the nostril. Toss a stone into the darkness; it goes on falling. What, then, of the winter, the blank rock tusked with ice? If it is cold in summer, in winter you can't breathe. I have stood in the pass at night and heard the wind shrieking on snowy heights, a shrill descant. There is no wilder sound, with the lakes solid, ribbed. The time of the raven and the blue hare, and the fox's track through the snow. The sheep are down in the green *fridd*[2], the walled enclosure with its scatter of stones. The goats come down, too, and the ponies. Nothing can live in that refrigerated air except the ravens. Already they are inspecting the frozen ledges, repairing their last year's hovel. On clear days there is their hard, resonant bark and the quick somersault on stiff wing. Before the first primroses in the valley and with snow still choking the hollows, there will be red throats to fill in the ravens' nest.

Who built the mountain walls, those long necklaces of stone? No one can remember their not being there with their shelter on bad days. As you go up with your heart pounding, using them shamefully like a banister, the quiet ewe watches you with her split eyes. The grass is warm and pressed flat, a traditional resting place, old as the worn tracks leading to the gap in the wall, where the sheep crouch to get through. There are bright badges of lichen on the stones; they were there when strong hands constructed the wall. They are so small and so old, nature's earliest colonists.

Keep climbing. The wall ends against a buttress of rock, and the scree begins. Here parsley fern grows and bilberry, where the sheep have not come. Further up from somewhere among the pinnacles four double notes are whistled high and melancholy, the only bird song likely to be heard at this altitude apart from the wren's fussation. This is the ring-ouzel's home for a few brief months. The hen sits on her nest in some draughty gully, while her white-collared mate makes the place more lonely with his song. The Welsh have a name for him, *mwyalchen y mynydd*, mountain blackbird.

And now the chimneys, the cold funnels of rock. Feet pressed to one side and back to the other, you work your way up to inspect some patch of colour above you, roseroot or saxifrage or the crimson moss campion. There is something spiritual in these high rock-gardens; the sudden rich colour in all this bareness, the delicate shell of a flower balancing the mountain's weight. How many have fallen to their death in reaching for the trembling petals just out of range? The eye fixes on the one blossom, ignoring the airy chasm. The higher you go, the more each stone must be examined. This is the ultimate test, when everything begins to come away in the hand. You hear, but dare not watch the endless shift of the shale. It is very lonely up here, and you are very small, but heavy. The solidest jags yield to your pressure. This is where the prudent man turns back. Ten feet from the top with only the moon's encouragement. The brave man finds a way round: a crack in the chimney to be squeezed through, a series of notches and ledges and he drags himself panting onto a grassy shelf; the sort the shepherd lets the goats clip to save the ewes from being tempted. A brief rest, and he is looking back down the ascent as a boxer looks at his prostrate rival.

And so to the summit. Five minutes later all is forgotten. The sun is warm, the air golden. The blood courses vigorously through the veins. What are death, danger? This is the top of the world and this is I; there is nothing else, no living being. There are no sheep here to run off with sharply intaken breath, like silk tearing. There are no birds, flowers. There is an immense silence, broken only by the wind, coming and going among the piled rocks and stones. This is what it is to be God; to have the whole earth at one's feet; to see lakes the size of hoofprints; to see large streams drawn through the landscape like threads; to watch swagging clouds go by a little over one's head. The silent watcher upon the hills! How are you different from bird or stone? Companionless, you have no responsibilities. Your function is to observe from the slow traffic of the clouds up the slope to the busy insect hurrying across the hand.

And then the old ache in the mind begins, the restlessness of the bone. You begin tossing small stones into a hollow, flicking them one by one off the nail. How many years to live? The blood begins to cool; there is formication of the skin. You get up and walk about, loth to leave yet knowing you can't stay. It is all self now: the needs of the body, the flesh anxious for itself. The exultation has worn off. A mountain top is a small place; one gets used to the furniture. Choosing an easier way down, you stop after a few yards and look back. The summit is still there, inviting as ever, with the clouds at speed. But it is a familiar place now, and carries its human stain. You turn with a sigh to continue valley-wards. And in the first trees a blackbird sings, ambassador from another world. After the astringency of the mountain such richness, such domesticity! Meadows are full of grass, brimming with flowers. The air oozes birdsong and scent, an oppression of the nostrils. The first man you meet greets you casually, as though you were not God.

Who lives in the dripping house under the falls? Pale people, starved of sunlight; lanky as things grown in the dark. Their hands hang down and their clothes steam. They eat mildew and green mould. Silent people; the sound of the water drowns all. Its diatribe fills their sleep. They have no bird music. The fish open their mouths silently in the deep pool: the clear grotto under the scaled leaves. Only winter can make it hold its tongue. The roughening of the water, the crisping of the spray; the glass tower rising from the floor. And still the inmates do not speak, scared now by the unusual silence. This is the house the stranger comes to; knocking on the door at night. No, not knocking, but a presence, there in the dark, making them open. He glides in, nebulous as moonlight. At the long table he tells his tale. "I cut the rope. I cut the rope." They eye one another in wan lamplight. On the blank wall he casts no shadow.

It is not good to live by mountains. They demand human sacrifice. Every year someone must die. The tall figures approach from the towns, heavy booted, wearing their ropes like a snail. The mountain endures them for a while. They dwindle on its huge sides like lice. The eye watches their ascent. For an hour they seem not to move, somnambulists feeling their way blindly. Then suddenly they fall. The monster has shrugged them off. They lie senseless against its thigh. To the natives it is no surprise. The mountain is not a dead thing; they have heard it breathing. Through all time it lies and waits.

You were tired after your long climb. Your limbs ached; you sank into a dreamless sleep. But that was not the end. You withdrew for a while, but grew restless. Other mountains rose in the mind, surfacing from old depths. They are as different as people, and stranger, remembering far things. Some are withdrawn; it takes long hours to come near. First the main road; then the lane, rising gradually, unnoticed. Hedges at first, with ploughed fields; squalls of gulls. Then the walls begin, with razor edges, blunted by wool. The last larches appear, bent backward before the wind; tattered schooners making impossible voyages. The lane turns to a track, plated with blue rock. There are twists of water, ticking away like a fast pulse. And now, out on the shining grass, where the slopes begin; the sheep mushroom plentiful. Alongside you the staircased stream with at each step the water's steel comb. The smooth stretches are black as tea, but the gorse is like butter. This is the grey wagtail's home and the wheatear's. There are no precipices here; you can walk at random. This mountain destroys in its own way. The *molinia*³ stretches for miles; there are no landmarks. Make your way to that small rise; it is not the top. Try that mound with its rock outcrop; you are no higher. Where is the summit? Is it that ridge over there? You descend into the long hollow and make your way up the far side, and the sun goes in. There is a clamminess in the air. Grey cloud hides your objective. You begin to flounder in the thick wind. Where did this pool come from? There are tall figures about you; old peat cuttings. The earth is soft under your feet; the ground moves, is unstable. There is a mournful wailing about you; the golden plover, crying for the lost traveller. You could walk all day in this mist, moving in circles. This also is mountain, *y mynydd*,⁴ the sheep-walk. The farmer never hinders you; but accepts no responsibility. He bends over his sheep, as you pass. Too many strangers come through his yard. What if one less returns? He could have come down another way. Meanwhile the bone begins to feel the cold; the fingers are numb. You thought there was shelter under this boulder. For sheep it is a warm bed. There is an old skull, grown green, and a tin can. Other men have been here. There is a sudden hunger for voices, for location, for identity in this vague grey. You should have spoken to the farmer, told where you were going, who you were. Anonymity is for the towns, the packed thorough-fares. The mist races endlessly by. There is complete silence, complete disregard. You have done this before in different places, sheltering from a shower, hiding from men's eyes with a bland assurance, ready to resume your life when you felt like it. There is nothing here to resume. The blankness eats into you like decay; the cloud keeps up its skirmish. You get up and look round and see nothing. The head spins; the eyebrows are drenched with cold. Then suddenly, like the light coming on, brightness and warmth. The cloud goes past like a train, lurching silently away. The day returns; the earth is articulated. Far down you see the farm with the faint track blurring into the moor. And other people start out to climb. You move off to avoid them.

That was one day. But there are many days, and the mountains are inexhaustible. How high do they have to be? They say to the heroine in the film: "Look up; higher, higher, higher..." And the scream begins. Wordsworth rows out from the shore in the shadow of the hill, and then looming, rearing, towering above it into the night, black and enormous, the mountain. But a hill will do, and you at the bottom, in a valley perhaps, with night coming. Or by day in winter a hill keeps the sun off, a frost pocket. The trees and hedges are rimed all day, the raindrops unpricked. Yet it's the real hills that thrill, the mountains proper; three thousand feet and more, jagged edged. At dusk they are like a cave, gaping, appalling. But luminous at the rim. Far, far up there is a light like a flower; some mountain man farming sheep on the wild slopes; some sallow-faced man with raven hair and long skull. His dogs listen for foxes. The mountains stand round in a crescent, stabbing the sky. He utters them one by one, like a prayer, but correctly: *Moel Hebog, Yr Wyddfa, Lliwedd, Tryfan, Moel Siabod.* Tomorrow they will take the sun, wearing it like a king.

You begin the same, but coming to the branching sheep-tracks you take a different route. What you saw yesterday you don't see today. But what you do see! If you hadn't taken these few steps to the right, you would not have found the meadow-pipit's nest with its five eggs, leaden against the flaxen grasses. You wouldn't have found the pink cranberry flowers, or seen the yellow-necked mouse crouching pale against the wiry heather. Today the ravens are not flying high, but sitting glossy upon the rocks, or following their shadows over the blonde grass. The ring-ouzels are restless, darting at great speed down the waterfall of light that pours through a gully. If you had not swerved a little from your course, you would not have frightened the hen off her four pebbled eggs. And the bright bush of hairy greenweed, small enough to remain concealed, had you not rounded that poised stone. This is a new way to the top, enriched with tormentil. And the view when you get there! If the other day was obscure, today there is not a cloud in the sky. Hills you had never suspected stand up blue to the east and south. A buzzard rises lazily on a thermal; its ringing cry comes bounding down the corridor of air. If you had its keeness of vision, you would see the voles moving hundreds of feet below. But to you the landscape is empty of life, as it was before man appeared; grass and rock and water, and the raptor circling, brooding over it with lidless eye.

Too close to see the thing! It is good to stand back sometimes. There are other ways of knowing. The people out on the plain, or over the Straits, in Anglesey for instance. The hills are asleep. They lie at their ease like lions, and are of the same colour. Or they crouch above the water, as if waiting to spring. And the scattered houses about them, like a litter of chipped shells. The seasons change, and the light and the tones with them; from winter's bleached grass, the sandy dryness of March to the softness of June with its purple shadows, the bloom on the grape. Then July, *Gorffennaf* in Welsh, the end of summer. A coolness in the air towards dusk and a curlew crying. The hills stand up clear and very near. Or a day of rain leaves them swaddled with vapour; patchy grey cloud smudges them, with here and there glimpses of slate blue, with a peak floating above them, incredibly high. Then, as the rain stops and the sky appears, the puzzle to know which is cloud, which mountain. The people watch them over grey sea, or blue sea with its ermine trimming. Then the first fall of snow, the chalky whiteness against leaden skies, or rose coloured at sundown with the windows angry. These people are too near to escape the cold. The wind skids off icy slopes and collides with them. The water is dirty brown like a ploughed field. The birds' italics speckle the distance. Or the long curtain of cloud is lowered, as at a play's end. There could be no hills there; nothing but dark land running up that blank wall.

But to live near mountains is to be in touch with Eden, with lost childhood. These are the summer pastures of the Celtic people. On the darkest of days there is that high field, green as an emerald. This is the precious stone that a man sells all his goods to possess. But on clear mornings how the peaks shine! Behind the dark hill, still in shadow, there is the golden grass, bright with dew. As you pass on the road, thick with traffic, your heart heavy with care, your mind racked with problems, there is Eden's garden, its gate open, fresh as it has always been, unsmudged by the world. The larks sing high in the sky. No footprints have bruised the dew. The air is something to be sipped slowly. Coloured drops depend from the thorn. This is the world they went up into on May Day with their flocks from *y hendre*, the winter house, to *yr hafod*, the shieling. They spent long days here, swapping *englynion*[5] over the peat cutting. They have gone now; the cuttings are deserted; *yr hafotai*[6] in ruins. But the hill remains, keeping its perennial freshness. Life with its money and its honours, its pride and its power, seems of little worth if we are to lose this. This it is that haunts men, that epitomises Wales in a phrase—the bright hill under the black cloud.

> I'r estron, os myn,
> Boed hawl tros y glyn;
> I ninnau boed byw
> Yn ymyl gwisg Duw
> Yn y grug, yn y grug.[7]

I don't know who wrote those words, but they translate like this:

> Let the stranger, if he will
> Have his way with the glen;
> But give us to live
> At the bright hem of God
> In the heather, in the heather.

It is to this that men return, in thought, in reality, seeking for something unnameable, a lost Eden, a lost childhood; for fulfilment, for escape, for refuge, for conquest of themselves, for peace, for adventure. The list is endless. The hills have all this to give and more: to the broken mind, peace; to the artist, colour; to the poet, music; to the brave man, consciousness that he has looked into the eyes of death and has not flinched, hanging upon the rock face with the wind clawing at him.

The mountain rises dark under the moon, and the stream rustles frostily through the heather. On a bare bough, the tawny owl calls, a long shivering cry, that sounded before man came and will re-echo after he has gone; a cry that only the mountain and the moon will outlast.

Notes
1. The peregrine falcon.
2. Mountain pasture.
3. Moorland grass.
4. The mountain.
5. An *englyn* is a four-line poem consisting of 30 syllables (10,6,7,7), each line in *cynghanedd* (see note on page 53).
6. The summer dwellings.
7. See note on page 25 for details of previous appearance of these lines in R.S. Thomas's writings.

The Making of a Poem

Conference of Library Authorities in Wales and Monmouth-shire, Barry, 1968, ed. L.M. Rees (Swansea, 1969), pp. 32-38

The Making of a Poem

One of the gifts reserved for age is that after you are fifty or so you really begin to believe that you are a poet, and you can therefore sit back and tell other people what poetry is. One error that some people who write about poetry make is that they tend to take one aspect of poetry for the whole thing, whereas I try to be catholic and allow that everything which is poetry has the right to exist. If I were an editor, I would not go for merely one kind of poetry. Whatever kind, whether it was in fashion or out of fashion, romantic or anything else, if it were poetry amd fulfilled those conditions, I would say it would have the right to appear.

The question which everybody comes up against is "What is poetry?" and who is there to tell us? I don't really know who is to tell us. One of my objections to the so-called critics, or rather reviewers and columnists, is that they do not show in their reviews that they know much about poetry, mainly because they nearly always go over what the poems are about. I suppose there is nobody more to blame than myself for this subject matter business since for many years I have always been concerned with certain themes. Anyone who has read any of my work will know the sort of themes which preoccupy me—the hill country of Wales; the Welsh political and social existence; the natural world; the struggle between time and eternity; the struggle between the reason and the emotions. These are the sort of themes which fill my work and I have been guilty of propaganda, in that I have written a lot of poems pushing these ideas at people, which is not what a poet should do at all. I am therefore on rather flimsy ground when I accuse these columnists of picking on the subject matter of a poet without mentioning anything else.

But for all that it is not right, and I have deliberately chosen this afternoon to leave it out.

I became rather tired of the themes about nationalism and the decay of the rural structure in Wales, and one of the gifts reserved for age is that I can now think more about poetry and remember all the wonderful poems which I might have written and never will write if I had concentrated more on pure poetry and on the technique of poetry without pushing these themes and propogandas; without strutting and beating my chest and saying "I am Welsh". I suppose if we spoke to any poet he would say "If only all of us could just be poets and nothing else, and concentrate on our craft and not have to bother with life and the world and problems and politics and so on."

When I have spoken in the past people have been terribly disappointed because I did not tell them how to write a poem. I don't know how many of you write poems, or indeed how many of you are interested in poetry, and you will probably be insulted if I say that I do not suppose that you have much time to be anything else but librarians. On the other hand it might be that some of you really write poetry and no doubt many are definitely interested in it, and that is why I chose at random the title for my talking, which is "The Making of a Poem". It is not that I was going to give you the recipe or anything of this kind, but I shall try to tell you what it means to be this sort of poet, because I have already safeguarded myself by saying that I do believe in catholicity, and do not think that anybody should be just any kind of poet. What bores me stiff in the average art gallery is that so many people are trying to be painters by following the current trend or the current fashion. If it happens to be the fashion to stick little bits of something askew with gum all over the place, then everybody must produce one of these works and unfortunately poetry, which has been moderately free of this, is now tending to follow suit, and we are at present witnessing fashions in poetry as in everything else. Once you get that state of affairs nobody can hope to be in the public eye or to be read at all if he does not put himself in that fashion, whereas if you have any honesty at all, you are just about beginning to master that particular way of writing when it too has gone out of fashion. You must then start all over again and spend another five or ten years trying to get into the next fashion, and all this of course, to me, has very little to do with poetry at all since, as I have said, poetry is a matter of technique.

The older I get the more I come to see how true a generalisation this is, and as you know the old bardic tradition in Wales was that sound and sense were fifty percent each and that meant that in poetry the sound was of equal importance with the sense. Now if you speak like this about English poetry you immediately find yourself in difficulties, because it is so easy—as Edgar Allen Poe, for instance, did—to get worked up about certain sounds and certain ways of singing and saying things—as Swinburne did—until in the end you have a kind of signature-tune poetry, and you have acquired a certain facility so that you can churn it out and switch on the music, whereas the sense hardly seems to matter. I feel now, in middle life, that it is the actual *craft* of poetry which is important, and I think that this must be said and adhered to because it would save us from falling a victim to those fashions about which I spoke. If a poet realises that it has been his privilege to have a certain gift in the manipulation of language (language being the supreme human manifestation) then he is obviously committed from the very beginning to a life-time of self discipline, struggle, disappointment, failure, with just possibly that odd success which is greater in his eyes than it probably is in the eyes of anybody else. I know that we are now going into a period when the spoken word is becoming of more importance than the word on the page, and although this might be a good thing, I doubt it myself as a poet. I feel that you can cheat; Yeats used to compose aloud, whereas I compose on the page. I am certainly not challenging Yeats, who was a supreme artist, but I believe that the inner ear which goes into operation as the eye runs along a line of poetry is more delicate and subtle than the outer ear. When I am putting things down I try them out in my head, so that when I put them on paper if there is anything wrong it becomes apparent to me. I can still, as it were, take the line up and read it aloud again and get it right, but the fact that it is not reading quite right to me with my eye on the page suggests to me that there is something wrong, and this is a feeling which I trust. I am not forcing this method on any other poet at all, but this is my system of working and I have grounds for believing that it is right in my case. This means that there must be some kind of music which one is after, and indeed isn't this what makes poetry memorable? Isn't it just the way of saying things which really is part of our appreciation of poetry, and the thing that makes poetry last through the centuries?

But not just the *way* of saying of course. I want you to remember always that I consider poetry rather like the marriage of man and woman. It is an inseparable union this marriage of sense and sound, of content and technique, and that is why I am against those reviewers and columnists who pick out a bit of subject matter and say "you know, R.S.Thomas is a poet who writes about country matters and that sort of thing". It is so very sweeping and so inadequate, and it must be very frustrating to younger poets who have spent a great deal of time working with their pens and have eventually succeeded in getting the work published, to find that the best that a reviewer can do is simply to say that here is a poet who finds his subject matter in the sea, or the mountains, or the back alleys, and leaves it at that. There is nothing to show the poetic excellencies or some of the little achievements of that poet in expressing in a way which no other person who is not a poet could express.

And there is the music which I was speaking about, although I don't know if music is quite the right word. I do know that almost all my poems have had their initiation in the first line. Some line which comes into being in one's head; a line with its particular stresses and its particular scansion, sets the rhythm and the pattern for the whole poem. This links it up for me with all that has been written about the dance of life, the rhythm of life, the music of the spheres, the eternity of art, and all that sort of thing. But creatures of time and space as we all are, we are yet haunted by dreams of eternity and we have a conception of ourselves as arresting the flow of time. When we love somebody, or we see something very beautiful, or when we are experiencing something very wonderful or very strange which has a dreamlike quality about it, there is on that occasion something within us which wants to arrest this and keep it forever, and we know that in so far as we are creatures of time and space this does not seem to be possible. Almost before we have really had our attention drawn to it either we have passed on or it has gone in the slip-stream and is no more. Most of us would feel that if only we had the gift of language, or if only we had the hand of the painter, or if only we were musicians, we should try to formalise and crystallise or trap this evanescent experience, and arrest it and take it out of the time-flow. And this is surely what the better poets are able to do.

How is it that certain lines come down to us from the past; man won't let them die because they are doing justice for him. "From you I have been absent in the spring...";[1] it seems a commonplace enough observation, but it was doing something for man which man recognised and therefore man will not let it die. "Ah! Sun-Flower! weary of time, who countest the steps of the Sun";[2] these are the things you see aren't they? Or again "the spirit that stands by the naked man".[3] This is the poet's ability to compress, and in the act of compressing to set up vibrations which will go on to whatever eternity of which man is capable. As long as language is spoken— whether it be English or Welsh or French, or any other language— these masters of the written word who have tapped these resources and formalised the thoughts and the experience into a poem, are the people whom we call poets. Obviously every writer, myself included, is trying to join that company, and these are the sort of feelings which I now have in middle life. As I say, this is the obligation which I feel is upon me—to try to experience life in all its richness, wonder and strangeness, and to use the best language which I possess to describe that experience: it is obvious that if this description bores me, it is going to bore other people too.

Some people say "What a pity you throw things in the wastepaper basket. Other people would be very pleased to see these efforts and read them". I do not hold with this at all, because in the act of creation the poet himself is the supreme critic, and it is he and he alone who must choose, select and reject whatever he considers is to his purpose on that particular occasion. Now I find that constructed as human beings as we are, in ninety-nine cases out of a hundred it is a failure. You think that you have got a wonderful idea; the line has come and you begin to work on it, and then you write a few more lines. Gradually it dawns on your consciousness that you just are not making the grade and that the best thing to do is to roll the thing up and throw it away.

And indeed one can do quite a lot of this. Sometimes, when one is most despondent and feeling "well this is the end, I shall not be a poet any more" and the best thing to do is to pack up and join the golf club or something, strangely from somewhere will come something which satisfies one. I do not want to sound complacent and conceited or anything like this; because unfortunately these very feelings also can let one down. I have gone to bed many a night feeling that "well I don't think Yeats ever wrote anything better than this" and then the next morning approaching what I have written nervously, and lifting up the cover and reading it again and seeing that it is not even as good as Ella Wheeler Wilcox produced.

One can be had very much in this way, but nevertheless, owing to our sub-conscious, sub-strata, or whatever people call that experience, or that faculty inside us to take in things and to benefit from them, and to choose the right things when we are not really conscious of doing so, it can pay dividends in a poet as it does in many other people. Because after you have worked and studied and striven to say a thing in the way you want to say it and have failed so often, you will reap the benefit of all that work and those efforts, and the next day, or the next week, or just sometime in the future you find that there is some faculty in the mind which enables one to say a thing in the way in which one wants to say it, and to say something worthwhile at the same time. There then you have the poet's task and this is what it means to try to make a poem.

People have various ideas and misunderstandings of the poet's function. Some people believe in a sort of inspiration and little else, and they talk to poets and find that they are just like other people; but they still say "Well, he's a funny sort of chap, he writes poetry you know, and he gets inspired every so often", as if they were to say that somebody rings him up from above, and says "take this down, old chap" and there it is. And the funny thing about all these ideas is that they have a grain of truth in them. I have struggled all day with a poem and found either that I had to throw the poem away or that in the end I never really thought much about it. It does not quite come off, and yet something that has come much more easily has been a better poem, and so what is one to call this except inspiration. The people who are most likely to be inspired are the people who have had the most training and done the most work. I have tried to remember that my first job is to get to my study and to set my mind in motion and set myself to work, reading, studying, whatever it may be, and then when a particularly interesting idea or thought or rhythm comes to me—or visits me—I will be able to take hold of it, see what I can do with it and attempt in the struggle between it and me to shape it to my purpose. This means that there is something deliberate about the poetic craft and that you can't just hang about waiting for inspiration. I think it is terribly important for me in my case to be able to go and sit in my chair at my desk and to start reading or working, so that I am ready to take advantage of an idea or a rhythm or a line when it arrives. I do not want you to think that this is the way of all poets because obviously they do not all necessarily work like this. Wordsworth used to like to compose on long walks, whereas Coleridge used to like to compose whilst threading his way through brambles and thickets. Yeats as you know used to walk up and down in his room, mumbling his verses or his lines aloud. I prefer to sit at my desk ready to seize on that line which comes my way, and say "Yes, this has got something", and then to set the machinery in motion and to see if I cannot bend the line or thought to my purpose, and if I am successful I will then have crystallised a certain amount of experience within a certain framework and within a certain number of lines.

Perhaps I have been guilty again of separating a little too much the poetry from the poet. Now obviously one of the great glories of literature is that there are different kinds of poems and also different kinds of poets, and although poetry exists as a kind of abstract entity manifesting itself in all kinds of different forms—lyrics, sonnets, epics and so forth—nevertheless because it has been made by human beings the mark of the maker will to some extent be naturally on the poem. We have a certain amount of what might be called automatic writing, like Coleridge's 'Kubla Khan', but on the whole I do not think that there is so very much of this sort of canalising—this idea of letting poetry run through a person without the person leaving much stain or imprint on it at all. It is the kind of person that the poet is which is going to leave its stamp on the poetry, and therefore whatever experiences or whatever kind of person the particular poet is will have a very marked effect on the poetry which he writes.

I have written as you know mainly about country things because it is natural to me to live in the country. Although I was born in this neighbouring parish of Cardiff, I have nevertheless been brought up in the country, and it would have been quite false for me to try to write about the towns and about industry. I might have had a much wider appeal if I had written more like Phillip Larkin, who could write well about what it means to be a member of a cosmopolis today, but nonetheless, as you see, it would not have been me. I happen to be a person brought up in the country, living in the country and loving the country, and I try to understand what the country means and what it means to live in it, and what the effect of urbanization is on the country, and if there can be any reciprocal effect from the country to the town.

I also happen to be a priest, and am therefore concerned with people as a worshipping community, and of course all these things are bound to be like ingredients in some of the poetry which I write.

As a priest I approach things in a different way from you. I don't
want to set up a dichotomy of clergy against laity, because I do not
think that this is valid, but nevertheless it is part of my function to
look at things from a slightly different angle from the way in which
you would look at them, and therefore experience crystallising
within me, expresses itself in language which is bound to have this
imprint; the mark of the person who wrote it because he was a priest
and because he was a countryman and because he was a Welshman,
and indeed a Welshman who was deprived of his brithright. This is
why the very fact of being an Anglo-Welsh writer has such an effect.

The sort of poems which Anglo-Welsh writers will write will be
different from the poems which an English poet will produce and
they will be different too from the poems of a Welsh-speaking
person. You cannot ignore these aspects but the danger is that they
should become too important in themselves, and we can easily reach
a stage when one is praising a poet because he has written a certain
kind of poem and not because he has written a good poem. An
Anglo-Welsh poet writes about the coal pit at Merthyr, let us say,
and it is praised because here is somebody expressing what it means
to be a Glamorganshire miner, but it is not this which makes the
poem important but whether it is a good poem or not. This principle
is in danger, in Welsh Wales, in Anglo-Welsh writing, in English
writing, American writing, and indeed all writing. In so far as we
yield ourselves to other motives, and other pressures instead of
satisfying ourselves first of all that the poem is good poetry or that it
is exciting or in fresh language, or whether it has music and rhythm
which sets up a vibration in the reader which gives it significance or
that it is something eternal or something worth saying, then it would
be much better if it were rolled up and thrown into the wastepaper
basket.

I can forgive poets, as I try to forgive myself, for writing bad
poems, but not for sending bad poems to the printer, and nor can I
forgive any editor for printing bad poems. This is a warning to any
young person, or even older people, who are dying to get into print.
It is some terrible disease which afflicts any writer when he is young,
that he would give his last shilling for publication. If only some kind
angel would say to him—as I have to say to some young people who
send their work to me—''Think what you might be thinking of this
in ten years' time'' I am sure that most of them would desist from
pushing incomplete, immature and unsatisfactory work on their

editors and on the public. I won't say the public first of all, because I think the true critics—I do not mean these reviewers and columnists—but men who have studied literature and poetry, are the people who do set up a sort of standard, and it is from them that the public must learn, and indeed I think on the whole that the public is guided by honest and acute critics, and imaginative and sensitive critics. If you want to be a carpenter you go to a school of carpentry where you can learn your craft, or if you want to paint you go to the Royal College of Art or some Art School. Again, if you want to write music you can be taught all these things, but you cannot be taught poetry in the same way, although they claim to do so in the United States. A poet has to learn his craft from the study of all other people who have written. People write to me and say "Who is it that has influenced you?", and I always say "This is a question I don't answer because it is up to everyone else to find out what influences are visible in one's writing", but I always add that I am in debt to every other poet who has ever written and whom I have ever read.

This is how we learn to write poetry, by studying the achievement of the great masters; and not only the great masters, because as Yeats once said, he learned his technique from a man who was a very bad poet. Often a person who is not a good poet has none-the-less hit upon a certain way of saying things which is interesting, and then a superior mind—a better poet—will take this up, and where the other man failed the better poet succeeds. I believe that the public guided by discerning critics, are never really wrong in responding to what is good in poetry, and this is what I try to console myself with for my own puny efforts. It is probable, especially now at the end of the second millenium, that we are not going to produce any more great poets—at least not in this kind of civilisation—and therefore we must all be satisfied with being good poets. If we can have good musicians, good painters and good poets and people who are still saying things that are new and hopeful and interesting, perhaps that is about all which we can expect, and we should be grateful even for that.

Notes
1. From Shakespeare's Sonnet 98.
2. The opening lines of Blake's 'Ah! Sun-Flower'.
3. From 'Tom O'Bedlam', an anonymous seventeenth century poem.

Introduction to
A Choice of Wordsworth's Verse
(Faber: London, 1971), pp. 11-19

Introduction to
A Choice of Wordsworth's Verse

William Wordsworth was born in Cockermouth in Cumberland in 1770, the son of John and Anne Wordsworth. He went to school in Hawkshead, then, at the age of seventeen, went up to St John's College, Cambridge. Vacations were spent in walking tours, in England and on the continent, generally in the company of a friend such as Robert Jones. In 1791, he re-visited France alone, staying until 1792. His republican sympathies brought him in contact with a young Frenchwoman, Annette Vallon, by whom he had a child. Back in England he, with his sister Dorothy, settled at Racedown in Dorset, moving later to Alfoxden in Somerset. A year later they were on the move again, and a winter was spent in Germany in the company of Coleridge. Then in 1799 Wordsworth and his sister took Dove Cottage in Grasmere. In 1802 he married Mary Hutchinson, and in 1806 they moved to Allan Bank. 1811 saw them installed in the Grasmere parsonage, but finally they settled at Rydal Mount, which they never left apart from various visits at home and abroad. In 1850 Wordsworth died.

Such are a few brief facts about the poet. We must now consider some other aspects of his life and work.

Wordsworth is north of England. He symbolizes the yeoman of England with its sturdy constitution and independence of mind. Although he was frequently ill of a kind of hypochondria, and complained often about his eyes, he lived to be eighty years old, despite premature lamentation over his advanced age! Indeed, his long and frequent walks are sufficient testimony to his physical toughness. Fortunately we have artistic records of his appearance; but although the older portraits show greater resemblance to the serious, kindly writer of the letters, the earlier portrait, the drawing by Hancock made in 1798, showing the large, fleshy nose and full lips, is more suggestive of the wilful, sensuous writer of the great poetry.

We have become accustomed to a dichotomy between the life and work of artists. To what extent this is aggravated by modern conditions, I am not sure. Daily life grows ever more artificial and superficial. Wordsworth, living in the country at the period he did, had ample opportunities for integration, and this he achieved. His poems were almost entirely about the environment in which he loved to dwell, although the tree of poetry which grew from this natural soil soared into the upper air of the spirit. Wordsworth is with Tennyson, perhaps, the supreme poet of atmosphere. He can convey the feel of a place with memorable effect—''The tall rock, the mountain and the deep and gloomy wood...''

> The bleak music of that old stone wall...

Yet the inadequacy of the description of him as a nature poet is obvious. Through nature he became aware of the joys and sorrows of the human condition:

> For I have learned to look on nature...hearing
> often-times the still, sad music of humanity.

Through nature, too, he felt:

> a presence that disturbs me with the joy
> of elevated thoughts, a sense sublime
> of something far more deeply interfused.

This is that quality of which we must take account when we consider his philosophy. For the moment, let us remain with his poetry. It is wise and proper to estimate a poet by his virtues, his achievements. But most people are familiar with J.K.Stephen's satirical lines:

> Two voices are there; one is of the deep;
> And one is of an old, half-witted sheep...
> And, Wordsworth, both are thine...

The justice of these lines is palpably clear, but whether they are of any real value is another matter. Wordsworth could rise to the heights of :

> central peace subsisting at the heart
> of endless agitation.

He could descend to the bathos of:

> Spade with which Wilkinson hath tilled his lands.

This is the question which has puzzled so many of his readers: How could the great writer of the one permit himself, not so much to compose as to publish the other? I suppose the answer is bound up with Wordsworth's theory of language. So many of his apparent ineptitudes he was unable to abandon, because they exemplified the linguistic theories in which he believed. The preface to the *Lyrical Ballads* makes clear what he was after in this respect. Briefly, in reaction from the Enlightenment, the often arid, often verbose formalism of the eighteenth century, he aimed at the natural speech of ordinary men and women. One is reminded of a temporary aberration of Yeats, when he began dismissing from his poems all the words that were unintelligible to the Dublin washer-women. Coleridge rejoiced at the many occasions on which Wordsworth lapsed from, or perhaps one should say surmounted his theory; occasions without which we should not have the great verse which is characteristic of him at his best. Nevertheless, this, I feel, accounts for that flat, rather featureless, often mawkish verse, most of which I have endeavoured to exclude from this selection. Such verse must have seemed to Wordsworth to accord with his linguistic requirements, and he doubtless regarded it with the indulgence of a parent for the child who mirrors his own weaknesses. Mercifully, there is enough of the other kind to maintain Wordsworth's position as a very great poet, the composer of 'The Prelude', the Immortality Ode, 'Resolution and Independence', the lines written above Tintern Abbey, some of the sonnets amd several other lyrics.

It is rarely legitimate to detach the content of poetry from its form, and it is no easy matter to say to what extent even Wordsworth's best poetry benefited from his theory of language. Nevertheless we cannot fully grasp the significance of his greatest verse without considering the philosophy of life which helped to shape it.

This is obviously not the place to go fully into the above matter. Many books and studies have been written about it. But we must take account of it. Wordsworth is like one of the later American Fugitive poets, before there was all that much to flee from. What would he have done today? He believed in the quiet mind, the

inward eye; the time for contemplation. The grandeur and peace of
Westmoreland afforded him the quietness he needed, filled his mind
with wonder and exalted his spirit. The simple dignity of the people
who lived there accorded well with his own theories of what life
should be like. As it emerges in poems such as 'Michael' and 'The
Brothers' that life is the result of the reciprocal relation of man and
environment. The countryman gains in stature from the grandeur of
the surrounding landscape; the landscape in turn is a fitting setting
for the simple human dignity of its inhabitants. This is a poetic
variation on the philosophical doctrine regarding mind and reality,
or, as Wordsworth puts it in the preface to 'The Excursion':

> my voice proclaims
> How exquisitely the individual Mind
> (And the progressive powers perhaps no less
> Of the whole species) to the external World
> Is fitted: —and how exquisitely, too—
> Theme this but little heard of among men—
> The external World is fitted to the Mind.

And if Wordsworth inclined to one side rather than to another in this
relationship, then it was to an attitude of ''wise passiveness'' before
nature; or as he says in 'Expostulation and Reply':

> Nor less I deem that there are Powers
> Which of themselves our minds impress;
> That we can feed this mind of ours
> In a wise passiveness.

Such a statement is in line with the belief that ''one impulse from a
vernal wood'' can teach one more than all the sages can, and poems
on this theme are mainly the product of Wordsworth's late twenties,
when his lyrical powers were at their height. The years that brought
the philosophic mind brought also a certain modification of his
romanticism, and his near idolatry of nature became tempered,
some would say adulterated, by orthodox Christianity or even
churchmanship.

It is not the purpose of this brief introduction to go into the
reasons for the change in Wordsworth; to seek to unfold the nature
of ''the deep distress'' which humanized his soul. Herbert Read
made great play with the idea of the uneasy conscience, which
resulted from the repression of the Annette Vallon incident. Others
have hinted darkly at the incestuous nature of the feeling which

William and his sister, Dorothy, had for each other. What is more generally agreed is that the lyricism and vitality of Wordsworth's early philosophy gives way to a less adventurous, less novel, more orthodox view of things, as he grows older, and that this is reflected in the increasing dullness of his later verse. It is almost impossible to refute such a statement by quotation, and certainly the great philosophic poem, which Coleridge wished on him and Wordsworth talked about, never really got written. What did get down in lyrics, in longer pieces such as Tintern Abbey and the Immortality Ode, as well in isolated passages of 'The Prelude', are sufficient to convey a very definite philosophy of life, generally acknowledged as Wordsworthian. And if Wordsworth cannot claim sole credit for its conception, he is yet uniquely responsible for its poetic expression, telling of a time when:

> we are laid asleep
> In body, and become a living soul:
> While with an eye made quiet by the power
> Of harmony, and the deep power of joy,
> We see into the life of things.

The life of things! Wordsworth was not a recluse. True, he had a kind of animistic relationship with nature, which was best realized when he was alone; but he was appreciative of human company, and many a one shared his walks or formed part of his circle of friends. As a student he undertook more than one walking tour with Robert Jones; and later walked many a mile with Coleridge or Dorothy, spending also much time with Southey, de Quincey and Crabb Robinson. He also conducted a fairly wide correspondence. Still not all his human relationships ran a smooth course, and one wonders to what extent the brusqueness and lack of human finesse, of which Lamb and Coleridge complained, are attributable to a possible preference in Wordsworth for the non-human elements of rocks and stones and trees, which, if less highly organized than a human being, are also less complicated to deal with. However, this is one of the inconsistencies in the Wordsworthian, as in most other philosophies of nature; for however much he insists that "Nature never did betray the heart that loved her", "the dreary intercourse of daily life" has too often disturbed our cheerful faith "that all we behold is full of blessings".

I shall not say much about Wordsworth's verse itself. The late eighteenth and early nineteenth century were not so openly

concerned with technique as later decadence has been. The vowel
technique, the striking imagery, the metaphors—they are all there,
but taken in Wordsworth's stride, as it were. His chief characteristic
at his best is, as Coleridge pointed out, the use of "an impassioned,
lofty and sustained diction", which is directly opposed to his
linguistic theories. It is this diction which gives us the great moments
of 'The Prelude', the Tintern Abbey lines and the Immortality Ode.
Yet in much of his poetic theory, as set forth in the Preface to the
Lyrical Ballads, Wordsworth was very consciously reacting against
the inflated and verbose style of the eighteenth century, the
"hubbub of words", as he called it, of Pope's rendering of the plain
speech of the Bible's "Go to the ant, thou sluggard". This, to him,
was very far removed from the "very language of men". And it was
to the latter that he proposed to return. And even if, at his best, he
failed in his purpose, who is to say how much the profound
simplicity of some of his shorter lyrics owes to the same purpose?

> A violet by a mossy stone
> Half hidden from the eye!
> —Fair as a star, when only one
> Is shining in the sky.

While on the subject of language, it should be remembered that
Wordsworth was a great reviser of his work. The classical example is
that of 'The Prelude', of which there are two complete versions, the
edition of 1805 and that of 1850. It has been fashionable to praise the
earlier at the expense of the later. Certainly the pantheism of the
1805 version was later toned down, with a possible loss of force and
originality here and there. Perhaps greater familiarity with one
rather than another edition prejudices one, but an introduction is no
place for running literary stakes. Let me just say in explanation that
I was brought up on the 1850 version, and it is from that I have
chosen the passages which appear in this selection.

Finally a word about Wordsworth's message for today, which in a
way is a non-subject, for a poem's message is in itself. One can no
more tear apart form and content in a poem than body and soul in a
human being. The medium is the message! The sustained and lofty
diction, the sense of form, the aura of the poems are their own
justification. They convey to us the thoughts and feelings of a
literary genius living in a particular place at a particular time. That
place was England; the time, around 1800. They speak of the peace

that is to be found in solitude, the sublimity of earthly moments, the movement of the spirit of man. They extol beauty and love and natural wisdom at the expense of a shallow meddlesomeness. They set a "wise passiveness" to nature above the need to put her to the question. They decry too great an indulgence of the scientific spirit, which "murders to dissect" and which would "botanise upon a mother's grave".

As Wordsworth reclined in a grove sometime in 1798, it grieved his heart to think "what man has made of man". To many in these islands nearly two hundred years later, it may be grievous to think what man has made of nature. It is the editor's hope that a re-reading of this selection may at least re-open our eyes to the price we pay for our so-called progress, and, at best, remind us where we truly belong. For as Coleridge said, "The medium by which spirits understand each other is the freedom they possess in common".

Y Llwybrau Gynt 2

ed. Alun Oldfield-Davies (Gwasg Gomer: Llandysul, 1972), pp. 7-25

[The Paths Gone By]

The Paths Gone By[1]

It is towards the end of the first world war on the Wirral Peninsula in
Cheshire. A small boy is playing on the shore. Across the sea to the
south-west, there are high blue-grey hills. His father points to them.
"That's Wales," he says. The boy looks up for a second and stares
at them before turning back to play with the sand. The small boy is
me, on my holidays with my parents from Liverpool. My father is a
ship's officer and we live in Liverpool so as to be near when his ship
comes into Liverpool from time to time. The Wirral is a great place
to go, and even when we're not on holiday, we can go for the day
across the Mersey on one of the pleasure boats.

I was born in Cardiff, but as my father was at sea, we moved
about from port to port for the first six years of my life, spending
most of the time in England. I was, indeed, a town boy, and my first
memories are of the parks and streets of large towns like Liverpool,
of myself catching a tram down to the pier head to meet my father,
or going onto the ship itself and staying in bed in his cabin while my
mother and he dined with the other officers. Another time, going to
one of the parks: it is the middle of winter and the lake there is frozen
over. A crowd of people are sliding on it. Near to the bank, there is a
patch which has not frozen. A clergyman comes into view, sailing
along like a ship with the wind behind it. Suddenly, to my
astonishment, he disappears into the pool. Others come straight
away to pull him out, dripping wet. He goes off, crestfallen. Life
carries on. It is nice in the park in the summer as well. The breeze is
full of the scent of roses. I bend over to sniff one of the flowers—but
something nasty is waiting for me there! Quick as a flash it's up my
nose, and I start to scream. My mother rushes over to me, scared
out of her wits. After I have blown my nose like a dragon into her

handkerchief, the enemy is revealed: a harmless little black fly! But I remember the experience to this day, and I still take great care when smelling a flower.

At the end of the war, when I was nearly six, we moved to Holyhead, where my father had got a job on the Irish ferries. I remember the day we arrived: a dark wet day in December. Is there any town worse than Holyhead on a day like that? The taxi took us along the bare streets to our lodgings, and I stared gloomily through the cab windows. But the next day came and it was a pearl of a morning! Everywhere glistened and the sea was blue as could be. You must know the old penillion:

> Ar noswaith ddrycinog mi euthum i rodio
> Ar lannau y Fenai gan ddistaw fyfyrio;
> Y gwynt oedd yn uchel, a gwyllt oedd y wendon,
> A'r mor oedd yn lluchio dros waliau Caernarfon.
>
> Ond trannoeth y bore mi euthum i rodio
> Hyd lannau y Fenai, tawelwch oedd yno;
> Y gwynt oedd yn ddistaw, a'r mor oedd yn dirion,
> A'r haul oedd yn twynnu ar waliau Caernarfon.[2]

There you have a fair description of the sort of weather Anglesey has. Indeed if someone asks you what sort of weather to expect there, tell him: Oh, it'll get better towards the afternoon. The weather was king in Holyhead. It ruled almost all my activities. I was a sickly child in my early teens. My mother believed that enough fresh air would make a new man of me. So for a year I didn't go to school; I stayed in the open air. I wandered through the fields; I played on the river banks; I fished for blennies among the rocks. These were *some* blennies too! I loved the eager way they grabbed at the bait. All that was needed was to put a piece of a limpet on a bent pin, lower it into a small pool, and watch the blenny charge at it from its hiding-place, to be caught by me and put in a jam-jar. I could have fished for hours, but an eye to be kept on the tide. I was caught more than once, and had to jump through the water to the shore; and then got a good talking to from my mother.

When the time came for me to start school, I met some new friends: a family who lived at the other end of the Island.[3] The mother was a widow, with three children, a girl and two boys. The girl was three years older than me, but the boys were about my age. They lived in Penrhos Feilw, and soon that name came to seem like

magic to me. The house stood alone in the fields with the open sea
about half a mile away. The boys had places in the gorse where they
could hide, completely out of sight—long tunnels leading through
the undergrowth to some central chamber, and there we would sit
like red Indians to make our plans. My mother and father used to
visit their mother quite often, and while they chatted or played cards
in the winter, we children would be playing in and out of the house.
It was a marvellous experience to sneak out into the darkness
sometimes and stand under the stars with the wind from the sea
sighing about the silent house. And then we used to walk the two
miles or so home through the night, with the gorse creaking on either
side of the road, and the occasional shooting-star speeding quietly
across the heavens and disappearing like Williams Parry's fox.[4]
Safely in bed, I would go to sleep to the sound of the singing of a
group of locals who used to gather sometimes on the corner of the
street behind our house.

In the summer I would go over to my friends even more often.
There was a good spot for bathing nearby, an inlet called Porth Gof
Du, and it was there we liked to go. They were like porpoises in the
water and I quickly learnt to swim. It was a perfect place, and
completely private. Very rarely would there be anyone else there.
When the tide came in there would be about six foot of water in the
sandy trough which formed the inlet. The water was crystal-clear,
and the fish-spawn and sand-eels stood out blue in its depths. The
inlet faced east, and on many a morning I saw the sea shining like
silver or gold in the sun. On mornings like these, our hearts were
light and full of fun, and we would sing at the top of our voices along
the path through the heather to the inlet. Certainly there was some
magic in the sea there, and the body cried out to be baptised in it.
Other times, in the afternoon when the inlet was in the shade, after a
quick swim we would get dressed and go to explore the cliffs. I didn't
have such a good head for heights as my friends and I would often
have to turn back, only to be called a coward. But I eventually learnt
how to look over the edge of the cliff without being frightened too
much, and discovered that there was a fairly easy way down after
all. It was a delight to climb down to some small remote beach, with
the cliffs like a wall around us, and to feel that no-one had ever stood
there before. And the seagulls would add to that feeling, circling
overhead making a deafening noise. Sometimes, to disprove our
belief that we were the first there, we would come across an iron

ring. But we would soon decide that pirates had fixed it there! Have
you ever heard the sound of the sea in a little rocky cove? There is no
sound like it; or like the hollow smack of a wave penetrating the deep
recesses of the rock. This was true solitude, and even three lively and
mischievous boys would become quieter under its influence. Then a
race up to the top of the cliff; sometimes getting stuck because we
had taken a wrong turning. The only thing to do then was to go back
and start again, although the top of the cliff was only a few yards
away. The perfect end to a day like that in the summer, was to walk
home through a twilight full of the smell of grass and honeysuckle
and the song of the nightjar in the bracken. My skin would be
stinging from the sun and salt sea; but a glass of water before going
to bed tasted marvellous, and the white sheets were smooth and
refreshing.

I have said a lot about my friends, but of course there were many
days when I was on my own, since I was my parents' only child. But
I did not feel lonely. I enjoyed being out in the open air, and I would
often be out in the fields before dawn, so as to have a few hours of
pleasure before going to school. The trick was to get up and sneak
out without waking my mother, who herself slept very lightly. She
had no objection to my going out, but if she had woken, she would
have tried to persuade me to go back to bed, to have a bite to eat
first, to wrap up warmly and so on. It was like stealing fruit; more
fun to get out without anyone knowing, and get back by breakfast
time with a whole lot of adventures behind me: having seen a white
stoat; seen the moon going down over the waves and the sun rising
over Snowdon. Having seen. Having heard. I very rarely walked
along the road; I always preferred to be the other side of the hedge,
with the result that my feet were all too often wet with dew or rain.
And although I denied it, the fact that I so often had a cold proved
that my mother was right.

One of the most enjoyable times of the year in Holyhead was the
mushroom-picking season. I was not the only one who was up early
then. How often must I have arrived at the good mushroom-field at
daybreak, only to see a dark shadow on his way out of the field with a
basket full of mushrooms. I was sometimes so determined to get
there first that I would arrive in the dark and have to pick up
everything white to see if it was a mushroom or a stone. And yet
those early mornings were full of magic. Have you ever touched cold
mushrooms, wet with dew, smelt their freshness, and tasted them?

"Frog cheese", the Welsh name, is apt. They have a vaguely cheesy taste, similar to Caerphilly cheese; a taste which disappears in the frying-pan, no matter how careful you are.

I have already spoken of some of my friends; but how did Rhodri come into my life, I wonder? After I went to the grammar school, probably. The Penrhos Feilw family were respectable and safe enough to make friends with. Rhodri was from the town, though. He didn't speak with a pure accent. He didn't get to his feet when my mother came into the room. So Rhodri was out of favour. But to me, he was like a fresh breeze from another world. He was not one of the local yobboes, yet he had no fear of them. To me the yobboes were terrifying. They used to hide behind walls and throw stones at me. They challenged me to fight and I didn't like that. If my father had taken more part in my upbringing, things would have been different. He had seen hard times in the old sailing ships, and he could look after himself. But he was at home only rarely in comparison with the time he was at sea, and so my upbringing fell largely to my mother, with results which were not to the liking of the yobboes. But Rhodri could keep up with them like a wolf with its pack. In the winter, when I was safe in the house with the curtains drawn to keep out the night, I heard sometimes an inhuman scream outside, and the sound of footsteps running past: Rhodri and his warriors on the trail! I once dared ask if I could go out to play. My mother became angry, and with righteous scorn asked: "What, with that lot?" I never asked again after that. I was allowed to go to school with him though, and to come home, and even to go out for a walk with him before dark. Rhodri opened a new world to me. His head was full of the fights he had seen in the cinema. It was he who taught me that the rows of foxglove were not flowers but wave after wave of Red Indians to be felled by our weapons: stones thrown—by Rhodri at least—with devastating effect. We would play ball on the way home from school. One day I kicked the ball through the window of a house. I was going to go to the door to apologise, but Rhodri grabbed my arm: "Come along, you idiot," he said; and off we raced. When we reached the corner, Rhodri stopped to look. "No one to be seen," he said, laughing victoriously. We went on, but sure enough the next day the headmaster came to the classroom and took me to his study. The cat was out of the bag, and my parents had to pay for the window. But it was Rhodri they blamed.

They did not like me being with him, though I liked nothing

better than to be in his company. His conversation was full of descriptions of the beating one of his heroes gave someone in a film. Those were the days of Tom Mix and his marvellous horse, and I occasionally got permission to go and see the cowboys and Indians chasing each other across the plains. There was one cinema which continued to show silent films after the introduction of sound in the others. There was a piano there, and I can still see the pianist playing furiously by the weak light of the film, and hear the notes getting faster and faster as the Indians overtook the cart with the blonde heroine in it. I can hear, too, the deafening applause of the town lads as the hero pushed the baddy over the edge of the cliff. And then to end the film, the heroine was waiting for him under a tree smiling radiantly. I suppose it must have been Rhodri who was responsible for my noticing girls. One of his friends sometimes came with us for a walk. I would see them turning round to look after a girl who had just passed, and then start to smile stupidly and whisper to one another. "Why didn't you say something to her?" they asked; "She smiled at you." It was a frightening idea to me. I was too shy to look at a girl, never mind talk to one. And yet, the little armed god was waiting for me.

There was another house my mother used to call at sometimes out in the country. It was full of children, boys and girls. One day we were there, and while my mother was talking to their mother, one of the girls took me aside and started to talk amicably about this, that and the other. Gradually I lost my shyness and began for the first time to bask in female company. I walked home with my mother as though I was in a dream. The world had been transformed. I went to sleep seeing two black eyes sparkling at me and hearing a soft silvery voice. The little god's arrow was firmly in my heart. After that there was nothing for it but to walk along the road, hoping to meet her by accident. Morning and afternoon during the holidays I could be seen on my way past her house. But I didn't succeed in meeting her. Eventually I plucked up my courage. I went through the gate to the door and knocked, trembling inside. A maid came to the door, and told me that the family were in the orchard. I went there and found the three girls with their father who had been ill. They welcomed me in a friendly and natural fashion and I sat with them under the apple-trees with the bees humming and the birds singing and the hazy, golden summer all around us. It was heavenly! I wanted never to leave. It was sufficient just to sit there listening to their sweet voices, and glancing now and then at my sweetheart. From time to time, I would also say something, just to show how daring I was. It says a lot for that kind gentleman that he asked the great lout to stay for tea! And this went on for several months while the fever continued. The shore was deserted, the fields forgotten. There was only one road worth taking. If I went to the shore at all, it was only to write her name in the sand! I do not remember how it came to an end—if it ever did, since some hold that one's first love stays with one throughout one's life. Certainly we didn't quarrel or fall out in any way. The whole thing just gradually receded from my mind, its place taken by other things, in particular sport.

My father was a good cricketer, and I took after him. If one is fond of nature, once can also be fond of cricket, country cricket that is—the fine weather, the smell of the grass, and the murmur of the wind in the trees. I was not so good at football. I was a fast runner and I covered a lot of ground, but somehow the ball would never do what I wanted. I never kept my place in any team long. It was otherwise with rugby though. This was the time when a rugby club was formed in the town, and I quickly joined it. In that game, speed is an advantage of course. All one has to do is grab the ball and run! But the problem, with a fast winger as you know, is to work the ball out to him in the first place. And without a good centre, it is all in vain. Being on the wing with the Holyhead team meant having absolutely nothing to do. And having nothing to do means cold feet! To be at one's best in rugby, one must warm up. So I did not develop into a good rugby player either. I never really got rid of my cold feet and after a spell with the second fifteen at college, I retired and returned to my old habit of going for a long walk in the country, to look on the beauty of nature and to think the long vain thoughts of adolescence.

Time passed. The time came for me to leave Holyhead and take my place in the world. While I was at the Theological College in Llandaff, I used to take the train home from Cardiff. As you know, the line from Cardiff to Shrewsbury runs through the Marches, with the plains of England on one side and the Welsh hills on the other. I was often stirred by the sight of these hills rising in the west. It sometimes started to get dark before we reached Ludlow. In the west, the sky would be aflame, reminding one of ancient battles. Against that light, the hills rose dark and threatening as though full of armed men waiting for a chance to attack. There was in the west a land of romance and danger, a secret land. But when I arrived home, I would forget about all that for a while. There was an English life to live, and work to do ready for the next term at college.

After being a curate in Chirk, between Wrexham and Oswestry, for four years, I decided to get married. The vicar did not want a married curate. I had therefore to find somewhere else to live. There was a vacant parish in English Maelor at the time, and since it provided a suitable house, there we went, into what might as well have been the English plain—that part of Flintshire which lies between Wrexham and Cheshire. And from there, in the evening I could see the Welsh hills some fifteen miles away in the evening, magical and mysterious as ever. I realised what I had done. My place was not here on this plain amongst these Welsh with English accents and attitudes. I set about learning Welsh, so as to get back to the real Wales of my imagination. I came on slowly, too slowly to be ready for a Welsh parish. I applied for two parishes, but the vicars refused to help me. I carried on with my Welsh, going to Llangollen every week for an hour's lesson with Iorwerth Roberts. But there was no-one I could practise on during the week, and my progress remained slow. But within two years, Manafon, a country parish in Montgomeryshire, became vacant, and there we went, to the Rectory on the banks of the river Rhiw. There was no Welsh in Manafon either, but the parish was up in the hills, and when the floods came down from the moors and the clouds flew past, I really felt that I had come back to Wales.

Manafon was an eye-opener to me. Here I became aware of the clash between dream and reality. I was a proper little bourgeois, brought up delicately, with the mark of the church and the library on me. I had seen this part of the country from the train in the evening through a romantic haze. I now found myself amongst hard, materialistic, industrious people, who measured each other in acres and pounds; Welshmen who turned their backs on their inheritance, buying and selling in Welshpool, Oswestry and Shrewsbury; farmers of the cold, bare hillsides, who dreamed of saving enough money to move to a more fertile farm on the plains. But it was in some ways an old-fashioned district. When I went there in 1942, there was not a single tractor in the area. The men worked with their hands, hoeing, sheep-shearing, collecting hay, and cutting hedges. The horse was still in use. There was a smithy there; I can hear the sound of the anvil still, and see the sparks flying. I can remember the

lonely figures in the fields, hoeing or docking mangles, hour after
hour. What was going on in their heads, I wonder? The question
remains unanswered to this day.

Manafon lay in a hollow. There was no proper village there, just a
church, a school, a shop, and a public house, and the hills rose
around it to something over a thousand feet. From the top of these
hills there were stunning views. Far to the north-west you could see
Cader Idris; to the north, Aran Mawddy and Aran Benllyn; and the
Berwyn further to the east. On a clear day Wales lay spread out
pleasingly at your feet like a table set for your delight. If Anglesey is
the place from which to see Arfon, the hills of Montgomeryshire are
certainly the platform from which to view the splendour of
Merionethshire.

Four miles up the valley, on the edge of the moorland, there was a
chapel the main language of whose congregation was Welsh. I called
on the minister to ˙ask him to help me with the language. The
minister was the Reverend D.T.Davies, and I got a warm welcome
in his house. And so I struggled on. Sometimes after a meeting or
whist-drive in Manafon, I would hear some of the people standing in
the darkness talking in Welsh, and I knew they had come down from
the small farms around Adfa and Cefncoch. I thought of them going
back to their homes on the edge of the moor. My dream would
reappear for a time, and the following day I would go for a long walk
on that moorland and meet some sheep-farmer doing the round of
his flock. A few words in Welsh and then I would have to slip back
into English. Had I been able to speak Welsh when I went to
Manafon, it would have been easier to get them to use a language
which quite a few of them still knew. Every farm and every family
had a Welsh name, but most people spoke with a Shropshire accent
using a strange admixture of Welsh idioms. But to someone with an
interest in language who had only English to express himself, it
could be a treat to listen to them. They talked about the land and the
livestock and the seasons; it was from them that I heard for the first
time the coarse but beautiful words of the English farmer. From
them too I began to learn the facts of country life. Their standards
were simple and obvious. Man was there to work hard on the land.
If the hay was ready to be carried, it had to be brought in
immediately. The animals had to be looked after for the profit that
came from doing so. There was not the least bit of sentiment or
tenderness involved. If a lamb died, the only thing to do was to

throw it into the hedge for the crows. Religion was for Sundays. And if there was an excuse for not going to church because a cow was calving, all the better. On Sunday morning it was more convenient, and more enjoyable perhaps, to see to the sheep, while in the evening, the women went to the service and the men stayed at home—just in case something happened, you know. But they were keen, skilful workers. Their hedges, whether trimmed or laid, were a sight worth seeing. And since the farms were on the sides of the valley, it was obvious to everyone how his neighbour was getting on. "Jones of Llwyn Copa has planted his potatoes." "Ffinant have made a good job of ploughing their five-acre field." God help anyone who bungled a job. The resulting mess was obvious to all. This interest in each other's life and work was inborn. I was often surprised at how good their eyes were. As I was leaving a farm, the lady of the house, standing at the doorway, would say: "Oh, Mary of Ty-Brith has already done her washing." I would look where she was pointing and there, a mile or two across the valley, see a line of clothes the size of a daisy. When a collection for charity came round they would look hard at the collection box before contributing, to see how much so-and-so had given. If a farmer with a hundred acres had given ten shillings, a farmer with fifty would give five. It was as simple as that.

There was bad feeling festering in the parish and destroying the social life: a dispute over someone's will; or someone had offended against someone else, by accident or design; and the trouble was often worse between members of the same family. Because of this, some activities were impossible to organise, since if members of one family knew that members of the other family were likely to be present, they would not go. It was also a strange parish to move about at night. Without moon or stars, it would be as black as pitch sometimes, and if one passed somebody, or heard people talking quietly at the side of the road, there was no point in saying "Goodnight"; there would be no answer. It was as though one was back in the old days of the border wars, with all the old suspicion as alive as ever. And yet in their dealings with me I found them very generous. One of the mysteries of the place to me was why they were so loath to give money to anything, including the church, and yet so ready to give me butter and eggs and other farm produce. They were very pleased to see one in the evenings. It was there I learnt that there was no point in visiting anyone except the sick during the day. From dawn until dusk there were endless jobs to be done on the farm. But after doing the milking, and feeding the animals, and locking up the hens, and then getting washed and building the fire up, they were ready to receive you, and welcome your wife as well. After my son was born, it was impossible to get them to understand why we did not bring him with us, since their children were allowed to stay up until their parents went to bed. I soon learnt that there was not much point in talking about religion and the like. The farm, personal life, memories of former times, and the weather—these were the topics. Then at a given moment, after some considerable activity on the part of the women, the formal almost curt command: Come to the table. And what a feast, for us at any rate. Their own meat, their own bread, their own butter, apple pie with a quarter of a pint of cream on it. And then back to the log fire on the open hearth. The women were all dying to get one of those ugly, modern grates, and we would urge them not to. It was lovely to sit in front of the fire with its ribbons of flame, without the responsibility of having to feed and clean such a monster. Manafon was quite primitive in those days. There was no water in the farmhouses, no electricity, no telephone. We in the rectory used oil lamps and drew our water supply from the field over the river. When the well dried up in the summer the supply to the house came to an end. In the winter, the pipe would freeze with the same result. But what was nice was to leave a farm after a friendly, enjoyable evening, and go out under the stars with only the sound of the river beneath us as we descended into the valley. After the brightness inside, it was not always easy to find the path, and the farmer would insist on showing us the way with a lantern. We would see the same lanterns in March during the lambing season. My predecessor lost his way completely one night, and after wandering about in the dark for a quarter of an hour went back to the farm for help.

In Manafon I came to see the difference between town and country. Pavements and tarmacadam make up the environment of the town dweller, but fields and mud are the lot of the countryman. There was a small farm on top of a hill, a long way from any lane let alone road. The farmer there fell ill, and his cousin, a lady from Shrrewsbury, came to see him. She turned up in the village late one evening in a fur coat and high-heeled shoes, with a large heavy suitcase. The shopkeeper did not know what to do with her. "She wants to go to Y Waun," he said, "I can't take her, can you?" I agreed to, and off we went across the wet fields and up the muddy path. The mud became thicker, and the lady more and more out of breath. I had to slow down considerably for her, even though I was carrying her case. Her shoes and stockings were covered in mud. She had come completely unprepared for the countryside, but I wonder whether even the journey on foot gave her any idea of what to expect at the farm. More than likely there would be hens under the table, and perhaps a baby lamb in a box by the fire rubbing noses with a cat, with a noisy lamp smoking and a pot of strong tea stewing on the hob.

I said that the weather was everything in Holyhead. This was true to some extent in Manafon as well. I believe this is generally the case in the country. One lives according to the seasons there. And of course there is more variation than by the sea. The winters were pretty hard in Manafon. If there was snow about, we were sure to get it. In the bad winter of 1947, our lane was blocked with snow from the house to the main road and we were unable to use the car for nine weeks. Some nights there would be a bitter frost too, and one night that winter we had forty-two degrees of frost. I can remember hearing the house cracking as the ice took hold of it, and by the morning it was impossible to see through the window so thick were the fronds of ice. Oh, how we welcomed the spring after such a winter, the first buds on the trees, the trout back in their old haunts in the bright river.

And then after a long, hot summer, the leaves would start to change colour, and for two months the valley would be like fairyland: the cherry-trees dark red, and the ash-trees yellow. There was a large ash-tree at the end of the Rectory lane which would be completely yellow by November. The leaves remained on it one autumn longer than usual. But there was heavy frost one night and the next day as the sun rose, the leaves began to fall. They went on falling for hours making the tree like a golden fountain playing silently in the sun; I shall never forget it.

And when the autumn came, the foxes would start to bark and the men would go after them. It was a strange kind of hunting that went on in the Manafon district. No horses of course, the land was too mountainous. No, they hunted on foot until they lost the trail and the dogs, and then wandered about for hours in the twilight. I often heard the sound of the horn high on the hillsides about nine at night, as the hunters searched for their dogs. There was something very odd about it, as though the "little people" were hunting for make-believe foxes in the clouds. But what a place for owls! On a quiet night with a full moon, the valley rang with the sound of the owls, as though they had all come to hold an *eisteddfod*—which brings me back to the Welsh language. The minister at Adfa left the area and I was once again without a teacher. But mercifully I came into contact with the Reverend H.D.Owen of Penarth chapel, on top of the hill between Manafon and Llanfair Caereinion, and he and his wife Megan welcomed me warmly into their home. It was mainly to them that I am indebted for being able to speak Welsh now. Progress was slow because of the lack of people on whom to practise, and one cannot take too much advantage of anyone's goodwill. But every week for years I imposed myself upon this kind family, and by and by, I came to speak with less hesitance and stammering. My first test came when it was arranged for me to address the members of the chapel. I remember the evening: the chapel with its oil lamps, the wind blowing outside, and about twenty local farmers and their wives, come to listen to this freak—an Englishman who had learnt Welsh. Mr.Owen introduced me, asking the audience not to laugh if I made a mistake. Then off I went for about three quarters of an hour, like a ship being blown this way and that by the wind. Somehow or other I reached dry land, and after some discussion everyone went home. I walked home under the stars, mumbling some of the old *penillion telyn*[5] over and over to myself, whilst the wind answered me in the hedges. When, a few days later, I met someone who had been in the audience that evening, he said, referring to my performance, "I was surprised, really". I went on my way in some doubt. I wondered what he meant. The peculiar thing about Manafon was that it seemed so Welsh, even though Welsh was no longer spoken there. Certainly people coming out of the public house late on the night of a fair would go home shouting hymns at the top of their voices. But they didn't use Welsh except on certain occasions. It had disappeared from the village school before the beginning of the century, although it stayed somewhat longer in the parish church. And of course this had been the parish of Gwallter Mechain and Penfro and Ieuan Brydydd Hir, eminent Welshmen every one of them. It was this, perhaps, along with the peaty river running past, which gave a Welshness to the area. Listening to the sound of the river at night, I often thought of the many rectors before me who had done the same, because Manafon was an old parish, its records stretching back to the fifteenth century. Indeed the earliest records were in Latin, before turning not to Welsh but to English. And even in the days of great Welshmen like Gwallter Mechain, English was the language of all the records. Some of Manafon's rectors had been quite well known in their day, but the parishioners' memories of them were amusing, That very same Gwallter Mechain for instance: Walter Davies to them. Although he was famous as a poet and Eisteddfod figure and as a reputable writer on agriculture, he was remembered as a sorcerer in Manafon in my time. The old men of the parish liked to tell me how he had a man stand on a stone in the river all night to repent of some misdeed. But when I saw the full moon rising yellow above Cae Siencyn, I preferred to remember my predecessor of long ago as the author of what many consider the most perfect *englyn*[6] in the Welsh language:

> Y nos dywell yn distewi—caddug
> Yn cuddio Eryri,
> Yr haul yng ngwely'r heli,
> A'r lloer yn ariannu'r lli.[7]

Notes

1. What follows is a translation of R.S.Thomas's autobiographical radio talk that was published by Gwasg Gomer as part of a series in 1972.
2. The translated version below was published by R.S.Thomas as 'Night and Morning' in *The Stones of the Field* (Druid Press: Carmarthen, 1946):

> One night of tempest I arose and went
> Along the Menai shore on dreaming bent;
> The wind was stong, and savage swung the tide,
> And the waves blustered on Caernarfon side.
>
> But on the morrow, when I passed that way,
> On Menai shore the hush of heaven lay;
> The wind was gentle and the sea a flower,
> And the sun slumbered on Caernarfon tower.

3. Holy Island.
4. The poem of that name, translated by Gwyn Williams, appears in *The Oxford Book of Welsh Verse in English*, ed. Gwyn Jones (O.U.P., 1977).
5. Old harp stanzas, often anonymous. They are generally in single stanzas of 4 lines, expressing the ordinary experiences of Welsh countrymen.
6. See page 106 for note on *englynion*.

7. This *englyn*—'Cyfnos' by Walter Davies (Gwallter Mechain)— translated by Anthony Conran, appears in *The Oxford Book of Welsh Verse in English*, ed. Gwyn Jones (O.U.P., 1977).

'Nightfall'

Silence brought by the dark night: Eryri's
    Mountains veiled by mist:
The sun in the bed of brine,
The moon silvering the water.

Where do we go from here?

The Listener, 8 August 1974, pp. 177-178

Where do we go from here?

Where does the soul go when the body dies? According to Jacob Boehme, there is no need for it to go anywhere. On a similar subject, William Empson says in his poem 'Ignorance of Death':

> Otherwise I feel very blank upon this topic,
> And think that though important, and proper for anyone to bring up,
> It is one that most people shoud be prepared to be blank upon.

In other words, over-concern for one's immortality could be a sign of an exaggerated individualism. One could propose the thesis that, where there is a sufficiently fulfilling life to be lived, worry about what happens after is *de trop*. For instance, if a national identity were sufficiently valuable, it would be completely fulfilling to live to serve it, and to die knowing that it would survive one.

Yet, in spite of this, archaeology has unearthed many examples of man's concern for survival after death. But other branches of science have made it more difficult to believe. The probes have gone on, outward into space, inward into the very marrow of humanity; and the reductionists' conclusion is always the same: life, the universe, man are nothing but elaborations of physical laws which can be subsumed under comparatively simple equations.

It is neither a priest's job nor a poet's to put the adversary's case for him. The world is growing grey, not with the breath of the Galilean, as Swinburne maintained, but with that of scientology or of an increasingly commercialised or prostituted science. "Art thou a master of Israel and knowest not these things?" This is the drop of bitterness in the modern cup. To be able to take a man to pieces and put him together again; to be able to realise power brighter than the sun; to be able to walk in space and land on the moon; and not to be able to answer the bereaved child's question: "Where has Daddy gone?" And our assurance, our "nothing buts" are always misplaced. We, with our veneration for John Locke, have our ears perpetually teased by Blake's singing question: "How do you know but every bird that cuts the airy way is an immense world of delight closed by your senses five?"[1]

Because of the immensity of that world, there will surely be many ways of apprehending it. We are fuddled with democracy: fair shares for all! "Ah, well, 'e's in 'eaven now," said the widow of a notorious rogue to the vicar who condoles with her. "I was never so near doubting in all my life," said the priest to a friend. Yes, it is the great good place that all are bound for: rich and poor, sinner and saint, healer and torturer, on some super Canterbury pilgrimage. And St Peter stands at the gate, and he says to a Hitler or an Eichmann: "Um, there's just that matter of the Jews to be settled first." And they say: "Oh, the seven million, you mean? Yes, well, I'm sorry about that." And so the burning, fiery furnace was invented. Can its temperature be adjusted to the equation between a homicide who was sorely provoked and a Hitler?

"A little water clears us of this deed," scoff the Lady Macbeths of this world, appealing to reason. But the heart has its reasons that reason knows not of. "Will all great Neptune's ocean wash this blood clean from my hand?" asks Macbeth. And his answer still wakes an echo in a million hearts:

> No, this my hand will rather
> The multitudinous seas incarnadine,
> Making the green one red.

So, in a way, it is the moral argument that persuades. The tough, the thug, the hard-headed businessman say: "I go my way. I do as I please. I make the world serve my turn. And when my time comes, I'm not afraid to die! Stone dead has no bedfellow!" True. If you are stone dead, you can feel nothing. So what is there to fear? But just supposing it is not true? Which is not impossible.

> Methought I heard a voice cry: 'Sleep no more!
> Macbeth does murder sleep.'

If there is to be any meaning to life, if justice and righteousness, as the Jews thought, are to be necessary ingredients in the divine make-up, there must be a future vindication of the innocent, who have suffered pain and oppression in this life, as there must be a correction of the arrogant and intolerant who have fed off the fat of the land here at the expense of the weak.

And yet, an uneasiness dogs one. Is not this legalism? "And Jacob vowed a vow, saying: If God will be with me, and will keep me in this way that I go, and will give me bread to eat and raiment to put on, so that I come again to my father's house in peace, then shall the Lord be my God."[2] This is man, proud man, dictating his terms even to God, and so no better than the scientist or the philosopher, who put life to the question. So different from the great cry of Job: "Though he slay me, yet will I trust in him."[3]

This is an age of searching and doubt, of confidence and hesitation. In the strangely shifting climate which is common to most of the world today, can there be a finer, more satisfying response than trust? The great hymn of the Christian Church, the *Te Deum Laudamus*, closes on the humble yet proud verse: "In Thee, O Lord, have I trusted, let me never be confounded."

There is no God but God. The very use of the word answers all questions. The ability to create life automatically posits the ability to re-create it. We die utterly, completely. Our bones are consumed in the crematoria. Shall the Creator, who composed this solid, fertile earth out of incendiary gases, find more difficulty in forming a new life around the nucleus of a human soul? The question is rhetorical. It can be framed in a hundred different ways. It was a cardinal doctrine of Aquinas that God reveals himself in accordance with the mind's ability to receive him. I have already scoffed at democracy. To one person, God may reveal himself as a loving shepherd leading to green pastures; to another as a consuming fire. I must end this talk, surely, by telling you how he has revealed himself to me, if that is the right way to describe the knowledge—half hope, half intuition—by which I live.

"When the sun rises, do you not see a round disc of fire somewhat like a guinea?" "O no no, I see an innumerable company of the heavenly host crying, 'Holy, Holy, Holy is the Lord God Almighty!' I question not my corporeal or vegetative eye any more than I would question a window concerning sight. I look through it and not with it."[4] So said William Blake and, similarly, in my humbler way, say I. With our greatest modern telescope we look out into the depths of space, but there is no heaven there. With our supersonic aircraft we annihilate time, but are no nearer eternity. May it not be that alongside us, made invisible by the thinnest of veils, is the heaven we seek? The immortality we must put on? Some of us, like Francis Thompson, know moments when "Those shaken mists a space unsettle".[5] To a countryman it is the small field suddenly lit up by a ray of sunlight. It is T.S.Eliot's "still point, there the dance is",[6] Wordsworth's "central peace, subsisting at the heart of endless agitation".[7] It is even closer. It is within us, as Jesus said. That is why there is no need to go anywhere from here.

Notes
1. From Blake's 'The Marriage of Heaven and Hell'.
2. Genesis, ch.28: v.20-21.
3. Job, ch.13: v.15.
4. From Blake's 'A Vision of the Last Judgement'.
5. From 'The Hound of Heaven'.
6. From 'Four Quartets'.
7. From 'The Excursion'.

Abercuawg

(Gwasg Gomer: Llandysul, 1976), pp.5-18

Abercuawg[1]

Where is Abercuawg? I am not sure whether that is the right way to
ask the question. Indeed I half fear that the answer would be that it
does not exist at all. And as a Welshman I see no meaning to my life
if there is no such place as Abercuawg—a town or village where the
cuckoos sing. So let me ask the question in a different way. *What* is
Abercuawg? And the answer here, of course, is that it is the name of
a place. And because a name is a word, it gives me the only excuse I
have for choosing to speak about Abercuawg in this literary lecture
which the Eisteddfod Council has so kindly invited me to deliver.

It is chiefly from the standpoint of linguistics and philosophy that I
shall try to speak today, but since I am a specialist in neither subject
you can imagine in advance what kind of mess I shall make it. And
yet here is a problem which is bound to stir the mind of anyone
interested in words. And perhaps the discussion will be of interest to
at least some of you, if it does no more than reveal the things which
excite the mind of one minor poet from time to time.

Yn Abercuawc yt ganant gogeu.[2]

In this poem of Llywarch Hen we are, amongst other things, on
the very threshold of *cynghanedd*.[3] And at once we see how naturally
the word Abercuawg falls into place in the line. We have heard
about *anima naturaliter Christiana*. Without a doubt, the Welsh
language by its very nature lends itself to *cynghanedd*. And this is
where the Anglo-Welsh poets, as they are called, lose out. They can
never introduce Welsh names into their poems half as naturally or
effectively as the Welsh poets can—and particularly the old
cywyddwyr.[4] Listen:

Y ferch wen o Bennal.[5]

Diachos yw Rhydychen
Am fod art ym Meifod wen:[6]

Na gwall, na newyn, na gwarth,
Na syched byth yn Sycharth![7]

And so on. There are countless examples. To one who knows
something about the beauty of the Welsh countryside and who loves
it passionately, it is indeed a disadvantage to be without the
linguistic resources with which to give it expression. And as is well
known to everyone who is compelled to speak English, it is
frequently tempting to do less than justice to a Welsh word occurring
in the midst of a whole mouthful of "yr iaith fain".[8] And, in this
way, many Welsh place names are corrupted and mangled. Be that
as it may, through using a word like Abercuawg, Llywarch Hen has
caused something to ring like a bell in my ear and my heart for all
eternity. Because of this experience I went in search of this
"something". I once lived for several years on the banks of the River
Dyfi in Eglwys Fach. Following the river bank in the direction of the
Mawddwy, I would come across a place called Abercywarch. It was a
marvellous place, surrounded by mountains, its bright crystal
streams singing like birds. But it was not Abercuawg, despite the
similarity of the name. I then read Ifor Williams' explanation of the
word itself.[9] Near Machynlleth there is a stream called the Dulas,
which joins up with the Dyfi between Penegoes and the town.
According to Sir Ifor, the old name for this was Cuog. The name of a
nearby mansion—Dolguog—is evidence of this. As soon as I read
this I went and found the spot where the Dulas flows into the
Dyfi—Aberdulas, or to give it its original name, Abercuawg: again a
very fine place. There were no cuckoos to be heard, though other
birds sang there. But where was Abercuawg? It was there without
being there. I had arrived and yet not found it. And thus there arose
again the whole problem of names, and words, and things, and the
connection between them.

This century has produced people who are obsessed with the
question of language. As if in reaction against the idea of a *lingua
franca* or Esperanto, they have marvelled at the richness and variety
of the tongues of man. Linguistics has become an important and
complex subject which continues to grow; and indeed it is true that
the power of words is a matter of immense interest. Samuel Johnson
remarked when preparing his great dictionary that he had not

forgotten "that words are the daughters of earth, and that things are
the sons of heaven." That is, things tend to fall in love with words
or, if you like, words are able to cast a spell on things and keep hold
of them. Primitive poetry worked somewhat in this fashion, and it is
this which lies behind the story of Jacob's struggle with the angel.
"What is thy name?" To answer this question is man's constant
aspiration. Remember Samson: "And he took to himself a wife in
the valley of Sorec and her name was Delilah".[10] And had not the
author of the Book of Judges told us that we should to this very day
be wanting to know her name. And thus it has always been. A boy
sees a girl and takes a liking to her. Nothing will suffice then until he
discovers her name and can repeat it over and over under his breath.
And the girls are just the same, mind you! The names of their loved
ones are constantly on *their* lips too, if barely whispered. In this
context, it is false to suggest that a rose, or any other name, would
smell as sweet. There is some kind of charm, some virtue which
belongs to the word itself. And yet, what is it? Does a name mean
anything in itself? That's a mistake that Englishmen tend to make.
My son's name is Gwydion. "What does it mean?" is the question
more or less every Englishman asks. He would never ask what
"William" or "Margaret" meant. Nevertheless, a grain of doubt
remains in my mind too, because of the inherent power of words.
"Now Gwydion was the best story teller in the world".

Our ancestors tended to religiously avoid giving pagan names to
their children, for fear they might exert an evil influence upon them.
As a result our nation was overloaded with names like John and
Mary. It puts a strain on one's belief in the immortality of the
individual to cast an eye over the old church registers and see the
number of John Jones' and Mary Roberts' who have passed over the
face of Wales like the shadow of a cloud.

Who deserves to live in Abercuawg? Not John and Mary and
William and Margaret, but, most certainly, Gwydion and Lleucu
and Rheinallt and Rhiannon. Some of you by now are smiling
discreetly, I see. "Aha," you say: "the cat's out of the bag at last.
This one wants to turn the clock back. He thinks we can live in the
Middle Ages". I wonder? We shall come to the question of time
later on. In the meantime what about someone like Islwyn Ffowc
Elis? No one would dare accuse him of trying to live in the Middle
Ages. Did he not write a novel entitled: *A Week in the Wales to Be?*[11]
Were the characters and atmosphere of that novel as incompatible

with Abercuawg as is the Wales of today? The Welsh language is in
danger. In the opinion of some, its death is in sight. And assuredly,
devotees of the Welsh language will have to ask themselves all the
more frequently in the future: ''What is the point of all this trouble
and sacrifice to keep the Welsh language alive? Aren't we becoming
more and more like each other every day throughout the world, and
isn't that as it should be?''

And that is the question which is bound up with the title of this
lecture. Because whatever Abercuawg might be, it is a place of trees
and fields and flowers and bright unpolluted streams, where the
cuckoos continue to sing. For such a place I am ready to make
sacrifices, maybe even to die. But what of a place which is
overcrowded with people, that has endless streets of modern,
characterless houses, each with its garage and television aerial, a
place from where the trees and the birds and the flowers have fled
before the yearly extension of concrete and tarmacadam; where the
people do the same kind of soul-less, monotonous work to provide
for still more and more of their kind?

And even if Welsh should be the language of these people; even if
they should coin a Welsh word for every gadget and tool of the
technical and plastic age they live in, will this be a place worth
bringing into existence, worth making sacrifices for? Is it for the sake
of such a future that some of our young people have to go to prison
and ruin promising careers? I have very often put such questions to
myself; and I am still without a definite answer.

Is this all a dream then? This is the human mind's eternal
problem, to know the difference between dream and reality. Renan,
as you know, accused the Celts of failing to distinguish between the
two. And yet according to Shakespeare, who was not a Celt at all,
we are all the stuff of dreams. In his play, *Antony and Cleopatra* the
queen describes Antony to her maid by giving her a long list of his
qualities and then asks ''Think you there was or might be such a
man/ As this I dreamed of''. The great dramatist left the question
open and it will perplex us as long as we live. Who has not had the
experience of seeing his dreams shattered? Branwen was the Helen
of Wales, wasn't she? Many of us, I'm sure, hold an image of her in
our hearts, not as she is in her rectangular grave on the banks of the
river Alaw in Anglesey, but as she was in her lifetime—the fairest
maiden alive. There are still a few Branwens in Wales. Did I not
hear the name once and turn, thinking she might steal my heart

away? Who did I see but a stupid, mocking slut, her dull eyes made
blue by daubings of mascara—a girl to whom Wales was no more
than a name, and a name fast becoming *obsolete*.

I use the English word deliberately. When I lived near
Aberystwyth I used to see Gwenallt from time to time and have a
chat with him. We would cover a lot of ground in our discussions,
trying to make sense of things. But sooner or later questions of
language and words would be sure to crop up. What dictionary did I
have? 'Bodfan' I replied. "Oh," said Gwenallt, with his sly little
smile, mentioning a particular part of the female body, "you look in
Bodfan and you'll find that it is obsolete".

What am I trying to say? That one cannot rely upon things. They
play tricks with us and words are our chief tools for dealing with
them and keeping them in place. But sometimes language succeeds
too well. So skilful are some of the great masters of words that they
create figures which are more real than reality itself, as it were. Take
Shakespeare's Hamlet for example. Is not Hamlet more alive than
the various Robert Williamses or John Smiths of whose existence I
have certain and unambiguous proof? Such a man as Hamlet never
existed. But what am I saying? Like Parry-Williams I am becoming
a little shaky. Was it not Hamlet who spoke those immortal words:
"To be or not to be, that is the question"?

Does Abercuawg exist? That is the question. And what is
existence? When I began writing I devised a character called Iago
Prytherch—an amalgam of some farmers I used to see at work on
the Montgomeryshire hillsides. In the opinion of some, he developed
into a symbol of something greater. And yet I had to ask myself
whether he was real at all. And there was something else that would
worry me as I saw him sweating or shivering hour after hour in the
fields: "What is he thinking about? What's going on inside his
skull?" And of course there was always the awful possibility that the
answer was—"Nothing". Nothing. What is nothing? I warned you
when I began that I wasn't a good enough philosopher to tackle such
problems, and here we are in the middle of them.

The question of nothingness and emptiness is too much for me.
My mind clouds over when I begin to wrestle with it. Welsh is
perhaps superior to English in this matter. "Nothing is nothing" is
an ambiguous proposition, to say the least. But "Dim ydyw dim" is
quite clear and final. What the English suggests is: 'Nothing is
without existence'. And in the light of this it would be possible to

assert that Abercuawg exists. But a Welshman can say "Nid yw Abercuawg yn bod". There you have a member of that race which Renan accused of mistaking dreams for facts. And now he is able to announce the saddest fact of all—namely, that Abercuawg does not exist! It is rather like those people who allege that there is no resurrection of the dead. Perhaps they are right, but how many of us can live with such a truth? Can we accept, therefore, that Abercuawg does not exist? Because if that fact is true, where is the process going to end? But of course, such shifting ground is a challenge to man's creative powers. One of the latest theories in the field of linguistics is that facts themselves are capable of being ordered and changed by words. So it is not necessarily facts which decide the course of a man's life, but words. And one example of this strange power words have is myth—man's capacity to create figures and symbols which convey the truth to him in a more direct manner than could plain colourless facts. What name shall we give this faculty? For many it is the imagination. But the danger is that so many people regard the imagination as synonymous with saying things which are not true. In order to understand its true meaning, one must be acquainted with the work of Coleridge the English poet and critic; and I have no time today to go into detail about him. It is enough now to refer to the chief tragedy of the poet's life, namely his loss of imagination, the creative power which enabled him to fashion things which come closer to the truth than did the common things of life. In his famous ode, 'Dejection' he lamented the loss of his capacity to feel the beauty of things. He no longer felt these things, but merely saw them. And yet this faith in the power of the imagination was the corner-stone of Coleridge's philosophy. It is not merely the mind nor yet the senses which bring reality before us, but some other faculty which is both higher and older than these, and which brings it before us *sub specie aeterni*, as Spinoza terms it. Or, in the words of William Blake: " 'What' it will be questioned, 'when the sun rises, do you not see a round disc of fire somewhat like a guinea?' 'Oh no, no, I see an innumerable company of the heavenly host crying: Holy Holy Holy is the Lord God Almighty.' " It would be blasphemous to claim as much for the vision of Abercuawg, but it explains to some degree why I am so unwilling to accept the kind of Abercuawg which facts would impose upon me. And yet there are plenty of people—a majority perhaps—who rejoice in the triumph of these unspeakable facts; people who, in the name of work or progress, or in the pursuit of large profit, are willing to surround Abercuawg with poles and wires and pylons, and to bury its fields under tons of concrete and tarmac, telling all kinds of lies in order to get their own way; people, who if the argument goes against them, fall back on the old cliché—You can't turn the clock back. But who in fact is guilty—not, perhaps, of turning the clock back, but rather of trying to stop it moving forward? In this context what Henri Bergson has to say about the understanding, or the brain, is of interest. According to Bergson, it is the function of the understanding to capture things as they are—to arrest them and prevent them from changing. If I understand correctly, he compares the mind to a camera which, in taking pictures, turns the smooth process of change into a number of discrete individual events. We are all familiar with the lifeless pictures cameras take, because their function is to freeze a particular moment within the flow of time, and to hold it for ever. It is the contrast with the stills produced by the old-fashioned camera which perhaps to some extent explains why people have taken so much to television. At least the small screen shows the world and its people and animals alive and moving. One of the excellent features of these pictures is that they show flowers and the leaves quivering in the breeze, and not still to the point of lifelessness as on a postcard.

Is change synonymous with life? Now there's a question! If we answer that it is, we appear to be playing into the hands of the promoters of progress. But we must be honest. Here we are very close to one of the great problems of philosophy, namely, what is the difference between being and becoming? You will remember the paradox of Zeno, the Greek philosopher. In discussing the problem of Achilles and the tortoise, he proved by freezing their movements into a series of small stages, that Achilles could never overtake the tortoise, because while he was moving from one point to another, the tortoise would also have moved a point. This was an insoluble problem for the brain, because of the latter's habit of treating movement as a series of individual stages. But to one who believes that life is a matter of something more than the brain, and who is ready to look upon change, or becoming, as one smooth, unbroken movement, the problem disappears. Or does it? I fear that I am trespassing on the field of the specialists again, and I cannot bring myself to raise my head for fear that one of them may be frowning at me through the window of philosophy or mathematics. But the

problem is a "funny" one, as they say in Aberdaron; and one which
persists in knocking on the door of the understanding. Have you
ever asked the question: When do a few become many? Take a
handful of peas and place them one by one on the table. One, two,
three-fifteen. They are still only a few, and yet a time will come
when there will be many. But when? At what precise moment do
you stop and say: There are a lot of peas here? If *after* fifteen, why
not *at* fifteen, or at *fourteen*? And the process is the same if you turn it
on its head and ask as you remove the peas, when do the many
become few? As I have already tried to show, the brain works
through freezing movements into a series of static frames. But in the
example now under scrutiny, the understanding fails to discover the
exact moment of change. It is overwhelmed by the nature of things.
The secret of life is beyond its grasp. And by the way, it is interesting
to note that the camera still cannot freeze the movements of the
adder as it strikes. As everyone probably knows, this snake can
strike its prey with exceptional speed. Considering the kind of
equipment which is to be had today, one would have expected
someone to have succeeded by now in slowing down the movements
of this little snake on film. But, as far as I know, no-one has yet done
so. And even if they do succeed one day, who would wish to live in a
world where the sound of bees is a series of small notes, and the
smooth movement of the sea is a pattern of small, static pyramids?
But that is what the brain wants to do—it wants to say: See. Here.
Now. It has this need to take us to the place where Dulas meets Dyfi
under the bridge which carries all the noisy traffic of the modern
world; where there are caravans and telegraph poles; where the
barking of dogs drowns the sound of the cuckoos—and to say to us:
Behold your Abercuawg!

There is something in us which refuses to accept this. Just as I
turned away from that Branwen, so we turn away from this
Abercuawg, saying: No, this is not it.

Abercuawg therefore is something like the moment at which the
few grow into many. It has to do with the process of becoming. It
cannot be grasped by the mind alone. And this, as I see it, is where
the Greek philosophers went wrong. To them, this process of
becoming or changing was magic and illusion. They were looking
for something permanent, something beyond the process of change,
and they discovered it in the Ideas, pure creations of the brain or of
the   Reason,   those   concepts   dressed   in   words   which   the

understanding uses to free itself from the fetters of the object.

It may be that there is some parallel between all this and the search for Abercuawg. The true disciple of Plato would say: I am searching for beauty not for beautiful things. And I am searching for the real Abercuawg, but I know, if I proceed along the wrong road, if I attempt to catch and comprehend it with the brain alone it will become ashes in my hand. In the words of that old Scottish verse:

> I would not find,
> For when I find, I know
> I shall have clasped the wandering wind
> And built a house of snow.

Is it then a matter of continuing the search? It seems so. And it is interesting to note that the great contemporary philosopher Karl Popper comes to much the same conclusion. So Abercuawg exists where the few become many, or the many few, that everlasting occasion which we can neither see nor comprehend, but which nevertheless compels our acceptance. We are searching, therefore, within time, for something which is above time, and yet, which is ever on the verge of being.

I am not qualified to discuss time, that mystery about which St.Augustine said: "If no-one asks me, I know. If someone asks, I do not know". Time is part of the material of our existence here. For every individual, it is something which begins with his birth and which ends with his death. It is irreversible. And perhaps it is upon this fact that the appeal of Abercuawg depends. It does not belong to some golden age in the past. Wales once had some kind of freedom; and the great literature which it produced may tempt us to overestimate that freedom. That freedom depended on force of arms. Professional soldiers fought against their peers and succeeded in reserving the nation's independence for an honourable length of time. That was the way of those days. The time of armed force is now finished, if civilisation is to survive. If Wales knows those things which pertain to her peace, Abercuawg may come nearer. What kind of place will it be? For an answer one must turn again to philosophy, or at least to Henri Bergson's version of it. You will remember my speaking earlier of the problem of nothing. "Dim yw Dim", in Welsh. Nothing does not exist. And yet one cannot conceive of this nothing. That is the mistake which the brain always makes. People tend to think that the original state is a void and that

being is something which comes and fills that void. We speak of
presence and absence. But we can never become conscious of
absence as such, only that what we are seeking is not present. Only
being is real therefore. "Nothing" cannot be conceived, as I have
just said. Try, You cannot. There is always something present. Fall
back on language. Call out: NOTHING! It is totally meaningless.
But shout: Abercuawg! and the echoes begin to awake.

This is what I mean. The fact that we go to the Machynlleth area
to look for the site of Abercuawg, saying "No this isn't it" means
nothing. Here is no cause for disappointment and despair, but
rather a way to come to know better, through its absence, the nature
of the place which we seek. How else does a poet create a poem other
than by searching for the word which is already in his mind but
which has not yet reached his tongue? And only through trying word
after word does he finally discover the right one. This is certainly not
an example of emptiness, but of becoming. And lest you think that I
am contradicting myself here, in ascribing some eternal quality to
the *mot juste*, let me remind you of the numerous examples in poetry
of words which were right in their day but which have subsequently
gone out of fashion, and have become not merely inadequate but
even laughable. This suggests that we shall have to build and rebuild
Abercuawg anew, as a proof of the fact that it is something which is
forever coming into existence, not something which has been frozen
once and for all. The danger that derives from thinking like Plato is
that we consider "becoming" to be less important than "the
eternal". But in accepting the process of becoming, man realises
that he is a created being. This is man's estate. He is always on the
verge of comprehending God, but insomuch as he is a mortal
creature, he never will. Nor will he ever see Abercuawg. But
through striving to see it, through longing for it, through refusing to
accept that it belongs to the past and has fallen into oblivion;
through refusing to accept some second-hand substitute, he will
succeed in preserving it as an eternal possibility. In what other way
did miracles take place in the history of the world? In what other way
have people ever succeeded in carrying on in the face of almost
insurmountable difficulties?

I have spoken already about how we become conscious of what is
right through its absence. I said of that Branwen walking the streets:
No this is not she. And about that Abercuawg which bears too many
of the marks of to-day: no, this is not it. We come closer to

discovering it, therefore, not through forming an image of it in our language, but through feeling it with our whole being. Have we not witnessed, in our own lifetime the Abercuawg which has been offered to us, forced upon us, its trees felled to construct a main road, its beautiful lanes straightened, its houses sold to outsiders? Have we not seen Rhydlafar become Red Lava, Penychain become Penny-Chain, Cwm Einion becomes Artists' Valley, Porthor becomes Whistling Sands and the Welsh accepting these things? Is not the "thin language" to be heard now at the heads of our valleys and on the peaks of our mountains? Have not our land and our houses been sold so that there are now no homes for our young people? Have we not married outsiders and reared children who have forgotten their native tongue to the point of reviling it? Have we not seen our villages rapidly become like any other village in the land? Is it not possible now to stand in the middle of one of our villages and imagine that one is in an English hamlet? Were not our chapels and most of our churches built as monuments to our corrupt taste and degenerate values? And did not the lazy ones among us say: There's nothing you can do about it. And the erring ones: We must move with the times? But a few, the true remnant of Israel, the salt of the Welsh earth, the people who are punished for speaking thus—they said: No, this is not Abercuawg. We must have something better than this.

According to Robert Browning, the problem we all face is not to see what might possibly be made beautiful, but to perceive what is possible and then try to make it beautiful. This appears to be a reasonable enough aim, in keeping with the optimistic, stout-hearted character of the poet who gave it utterance. But I fear that it is *too* reasonable. Here you have the cry of the compromisers. They believe that the only way to bring Abercuawg into existence, or to defend it subsequently, is by not interfering with contemporary developments, but rather seeking to channel them towards good ends. But it is not through compromise that we shall arrive at Abercuawg. And bilingualism (since we are speaking of language) is compromise.If the proponents of bilingulism get their way, we shall have to have an English version on the signpost which points to Abercuawg, and that will have to be above the Welsh of course! But the truth is that one cannot translate it, any more than one can translate *cynghanedd*. And it will not be a forest of poles and pylons, but a leafy wood. And the poles will be tastefully placed out of sight, remembering that it is man's spirit, and not profit, which comes first, and that the cuckoos will never sing on the ugly pylons of our teetering civilisation.

Notes

1. This is a translation of the literary address that R.S.Thomas delivered in Welsh at the National Eisteddfod in 1976.
2. From *Canu Llywarch Hen*: "In Abercuawg the cuckoos sing".
3. See page 53 for note on *cynghanedd*.
4. Poets who composed *cywyddau*—poems made up of rhymed couplets, each line incorporating *cynghanedd* (see above) within its seven syllables; one line in each couplet ends with a stressed syllable and the other ends with an unstressed syllable.
5. From Llywellyn Goch ap Meurig Hen's 'Marwnad Lleucu Llwyd': "The fair maid from Pennal".
6. From a *cywydd* (see above) to the Abbot of Strata Florida attributed to Ieuan Deulwyn: "Oxford is not needed since there is learning in fair Meifod".
7. From Iolo Goch's 'Llys Owain Glyndwr yn Sycharth': "Nor lack, nor famine, nor shame, nor thirst ever in Sycharth".
8. The thin language.
9. This explanation can be found in Ifor Williams' notes in *Canu Llywarch Hen* (U.W.P.: Cardiff, 1935).
10. Judges, ch.16: v.4.
11. Islwyn Ffowc Elis, *Wythnos yng Nghymru Fydd (Plaid Cymru: Cardiff, 1957).*

The Creative Writer's Suicide

Planet, 41 (1978), pp. 30-33

The Creative Writer's Suicide

In his book, *The Present Age*, Kierkegaard posed a profound and important question: Does man have a right to let himself be killed for the sake of the truth? For Kierkegaard there were three stages in the development of the personality, namely the aesthetic, the moral, and the religious, and in accordance with this belief he gave up any poetic ambitions he had early in his life, lest they stand between him and the religious life. And because he asked the above question in a religious context, it is obvious that I dare not discuss it directly on this occasion. It will be enough to say that he related the question to the crucifixion of Jesus Christ. As a divine person, was it right for Christ to allow the Jews to be guilty of putting him to death? God forbid that I should be guilty of blasphemy, but I should like to use Kierkegaard's question as a springboard for this address.[1]

After freeing myself from the task of speaking as a theologian, however, it would be just as easy for me to fall into the temptation of speaking as a philosopher by going after the word "truth". But then we are all familiar with the scornful question of Pontius Pilate. It is therefore better to let the philosophers chew that one over. And yet while I lay no claim to being a philosopher, I should say one thing, in recognition of the *petitio principii*: each and every person must interpret and pursue truth according to his own lights. This is not to deny the existence of one fundamental truth; it means rather that there is one truth for the biologist, another for the economist, another for the creative writer, and so on. Are these but aspects of the one fundamental truth? I cannot answer that one. But for a few minutes this afternoon let me concentrate on the creative writer, asking in the first place what is the truth as far as he is concerned?

The answer, I believe, is that there is a level of excellence that must be aimed at, come what may. His duty, his function, that which justifies his very existence, is to use every literary gift in his possession in order to create, in words and with words, a masterpiece. That is the truth for him. And in pursuit of this truth he is prepared to expend all his resources until he has exhausted himself.

That is how I would tend to answer the question of members of the general public who are so keen to know how a poem is created, whether by inspiration or after hours of hard labour. It is true, of course, that different writers work in different ways, and that every writer is not prepared to divulge his secret. Some can be positively arbitrary in answering such a question. If you suggest that good writing is a matter chiefly of inspiration, their tendency will be to emphasize the hard work involved. If, on the other hand, you suggest that a certain poem has caused them a lot of trouble, they will reject the suggestion out of hand in order to show themselves to be men of inspiration. I do not want to deny for a moment that there is such a thing as inspiration to help the writer to work better from time to time. But we have also the testimony of many an honest writer to the hard work without which the muse is rendered impotent. This may be taken to extremes sometimes, as in the case of Flaubert, who would choose a new piece of paper for each sentence. Paper must have been a bit cheaper in those days! But we know, too, of the scores of versions of just one poem that a poet like Yeats would make, not to mention many other lesser-known poets. A true artist is prepared to bear all this, as long as he enjoys freedom to practise his craft. The only question that may arise here is: how free has he ever been?

This brings us to the question of pressure on the creative writer, pressure which has been experienced down the centuries. Kierkegaard defined a poet as one who suffers. It is in his anguish that he opens his mouth, but the sound which comes out is so sweet to the ears of his listeners that they press him to sing again, that is to suffer still further.

Here we see the first temptation for the creative writer to commit suicide, namely by writing those things which tickle the public's fancy, in order to secure reward or praise, rather than those things he really wants to write. Who is not aware of the tricks in which a writer is prepared to indulge for the sake of public applause, until he loses every mite of originality that once belonged to him? And yet this too is debatable, because if he is a great enough writer he can compose a masterpiece yet please the public at the same time, as Shakespeare did in his plays and as the Welsh *cwyddwyr* did in their *cwyddau gofyn*.[2] It is a matter of how intelligent and cultured the public itself is. Where a public proves itself to be such, a writer may make a living and still retain his literary stature. Where these conditions are not fulfilled, his only choice is to make his money in another way, trying to follow the muse in his spare time, or to commit suicide as a writer.

But so far I have been generalizing, taking it for granted that circumstances remain more or less similar in every country, and that every writer is a member if an independent nation with its own language, and that that language is sufficient for every demand placed upon it. But what is the situation in Wales? You know as well as I do, or at least you ought to know. This devilish bilingualism! O, I know about all the arguments in favour of it: how it enriches one's personality, how it sharpens one's mind, how it enables one to enjoy the best of two worlds and so on. Very likely. But to anyone in Wales who desires to write, it is a millstone around his neck. That is, I agree with those who claim that the best literature comes from a monoglot nation. It is true that there are still writers in Wales who are fortunate enough to have Welsh as their mother-tongue, but these too are under pressure. There is not one of them who cannot speak English. In our present technological, industrial, world, it can be argued that English is a richer language, a language more suited than Welsh to the thousands of demands made upon it. Welsh is making a fair job of it. But what Welshman is there who has not blushed on discovering that so many words which he had always considered Welsh were in truth derived from English? What Welshman is there who is not ashamed at the number of English words which have set up residence in our language? Think of the *englynion*[3] and the jokes which depend on an English word for their effect. Welsh is full of them. If he were honest, what Welsh writer is there who would not confess to being tempted to write in English for some reason or another. And were he to yield to the temptation, this would be yet another example of suicide. He need not be disheartened, I hasten to add. Science, technology, and similar fields are responsible for most of the new English words which have to be translated into Welsh, but it is precisely because of this increase in the number of technical terms that English poets have so far failed to achieve any poetry of importance with them. And I am doubtful whether they will ever succeed, either.

Nevertheless, that is not the only, nor the worst, temptation for the Welsh creative writer. Welsh culture, which to a large extent is synonymous with the Welsh language, stands in danger of its very existence, as you know. In order to save that culture the writer is under pressure to write books and to contribute articles which do not represent his work at its best. But in so doing, he may congratulate himself that he has been the means of saving his nation from death, while at the same time committing suicide as a true writer. This is a problem peculiar to a small nation in a period of crisis, because in such a nation it is the writers who are among those most perceptive and most aware of what is happening. It is they, therefore, who are most sensitive to the true need of the nation. This can lead to sitting on committees, to travelling, to speaking at meetings, and so on: honourable work no doubt, but not the work of a writer, because for one thing it deprives him of his time, the most priceless item he has. How many promising writers in Wales have committed literary suicide or have suppressed their true talent by choosing to respond to these demands rather than to the demands of their craft? We were warned years ago by Saunders Lewis that we should expect from a writer or a scholar only those things which nobody else can give us.

Well, this is true enough and sad enough, but when we come to the Anglo-Welsh, as they are called (for the sake of convenience only, remember), the situation is far, far worse. An Anglo-Welsh writer is neither one thing nor the other. He keeps going in a no-man's land between two cultures. For various reasons he is obliged to write in English. Whatever may be said to the contrary, therefore, he is contributing to English culture, and deserves the strictures of his fellow-Welshmen on that account. If he endeavours to make his work more Welsh, he either gains the hostility of his English readers or loses their interest. There is no means of avoiding the former, and to get round the latter he has to resort to countless foot-notes, such as you find in the work of David Jones, which destroys the whole effect, especially in the case of poetry. Woe that I was born! Who has suffered, if I have not suffered? For I bear in my body the marks of this conflict. Who in fact is this vaunted Anglo-Welshman—one who knows that he is Welsh, or likes to think of himself as such, but is constantly conscious of the fact that he speaks a foreign language?

The north Walian is perhaps more conscious of this than his southern compatriot, who hears English around and about him every hour of the day and every day of the week. A foreign language! Yes. Let nobody imagine that because there is so much English everywhere in Wales it is not a foreign language. Should it not strike more and more of us that it is an abomination that people whose names are Morgan and Megan and who lived in houses called *Nant-y-Grisial* or *Y Gelli* speak English and are being conditioned to think like Englishmen. Aberdaron may have its weaknesses, but it is perfectly natural, while I am chatting to one of the small farmers there, for me to hear him turn to his daughter and say "Buddug, dos i nôl yr oen bach 'na". Yes indeed. If the Anglo-Welsh writer were only honest with himself, he would have to admit that he writes in a foreign language. If he is a true Welshman, one who is sensitive to the feeling and the traditions of his own country and nation, he will have some desire to learn Welsh in order to take possession of his true birth-right. Very good! But that is not the end of the matter. The desire then comes to write in Welsh in order to prove to himself and to the public that he is a true Welshman. Vanity of vanities. There are indeed examples of authors who have written prose of high quality in a foreign language, as Conrad did. But where are the poets who have composed truly great poems in a foreign language? If the Anglo-Welshman was not sufficiently fortunate to gain Welsh as a second language when he was young enough, and to live in a truly Welsh environment, he will never become as good a writer in that language as he could be in English. And yet the tempter is devilishly devious, and persuasive—showing how morally acceptable is the sacrifice. But what has morality to do with inspired literature?

We'll leave that question: an Anglo-Welshman who has experienced something of the magic of English as a medium of poetry is hardly likely to yield to this temptation to commit suicide. The English language does its work thoroughly. Thanks to his upbringing, the Anglo-Welshman will prefer English literature. Speaking personally for a moment I must confess, for example, that I cannot derive much satisfaction from Welsh *vers libre*. Is that because Welsh is not as suited to that form as it is English, or is it some defect in me? Whatever the truth of the matter, because the English language is rooted in his subconscious, as it were, the Anglo-Welshman has an instinct which enables him to criticize his own writing in that language. But when it comes to writing in Welsh he is unsure of himself, and consequently dependent on others for criticism and correction. It is too often forgotten, I believe, that self-criticism is a part of the creative process, and that anybody who is unable to do this thoroughly and directly is certain to fail as a writer, and particularly as a poet. That is my main reason for not writing poetry in Welsh. Because I was thirty years old before I began to learn Welsh seriously, and because I lacked the privilege of being brought up in a Welsh environment, I have neither the instinct nor the confidence which are essential for anyone who wishes to use language in the most skilful way possible, namely in writing poetry. I have therefore refused to commit suicide as a writer, but if you want an adjective to accompany the word "writer" I find myself at a painful loss. I have tried to steep myself in the history and traditions of Wales, but I am quite conscious of the way in which the contemporary cosmopolitan world has shattered these traditions. Yet I am just as conscious of the danger of a small country congratulating its writers for the sole reason that they write in the mother-tongue. Please forgive the Anglo-Welsh if they are able to see this more clearly than the Welsh themselves.

But all this is really a case of huffing and puffing while standing still! In the Wales in which we live, there is no literary answer to the literary problem. The crisis which is disturbing the nation is caused by political pressure; it must therefore be resolved politically. If you have kept Kierkegaard's question in mind while I have been speaking, you will have seen its relevance. He asked how could Jesus Christ allow the Jews to be guilty of what in one sense was his own suicide. I often ask myself: how can the Welsh people be so indifferent? How can they put up with conditions which require their writers to commit suicide? Every civilized country takes delight in its writers. If a writer is to be tempted to commit suicide, the pressure to do so should arise from within him rather than from without.

Notes
1. This lecture was delivered in Welsh at the 1977 annual rally of the Department of Extra-Mural Studies, University College of Wales, Aberystwyth. The Welsh text has been published in *Taliesin*, 35 (1977), 109-113.
2. Poems, using the format of *cywyddau* (see note on page 166), in which the poet addressed another person asking for a favour.
3. See page 106 for note on *englynion*.

Review of *Bury My Heart at Wounded Knee*
by Dee Brown

Planet, 41 (1978), p. 111

Review of *Bury My Heart at Wounded Knee*[1]

More than likely some of you will already have come across a book bearing the above title. It first appeared some years ago, but here it is now in paper-back. It is a record of the efforts of the Red Indians to keep their independence in the face of attacks on them by the white man between 1805 and 1890. The story is told from the Indians' point of view, but the author, Dee Brown, quoting from official documents, gives plenty of evidence for the truth of her story. I chose to write about this book, not just because of its general interest, but because of its particular appeal to us, the Welsh-speaking Welsh.

There is a romantic aura about the Red Indians. Many of my generation will remember going to the cinema as children to see exciting battles with the Indians. But as far as I can remember, it was always the Cowboys, the pioneers, who were the heroes. The Indians were savages, launching unprovoked attacks on the white men. We sympathised with the tough, honest cowboy, who referred to them as ''savage varmits'' as he decided to avenge some awful, barbaric unprovoked attack. It was the point of view of the white man, the American pioneer, which was put before us most often, and looking back I must confess that I too accepted that point of view. Nevertheless, I can remember how I used to indentify secretly with the Indians. They were the expert horsemen. They were the ones who were free and lived closest to nature. And that is one of the things emphasised in this book. The redskin respected the earth. Although he hunted, he did so for food and clothing. He never killed for the sake of killing. He would never damage the living earth. To an age such as our own which is beginning to wake up to the need to look after the environment, the Red Indians appear in a new light, as environmentalists. It was the white man who destroyed the great herds of bison. Between 1872 and 1874 over three million bison were killed and their bodies left to rot on the plains. Much of the forest was cleared or burnt just so as to put an end to the Indians' way of life and force them to go and live in the completely unsuitable areas which had been provided for them. The Indians were unable to understand how the white men could be so stupid as to waste the earth's resources in such a fashion. Neither could they understand the tricks of the white lawyers who drew up complicated deeds and documents to prove that the Indians had transferred part of their lands to the Americans. They understood that the earth belonged to no-one but God, the Great Spirit. They looked on with some scorn therefore as the pioneers rushed to claim pieces of land for themselves.

In complete contradiction of my original picture of the Indians as perpetually attacking the white man, this book quotes many of the chiefs to show they were not antagonistic to the white man at all. They were indeed too friendly, as they eventually learned, but too late. At the beginning of the century more than one party of pioneers ran into trouble in the hard weather and the Indians saved them every time. And even when the pressure on the Indians really began after the Civil War, they continued to say that they had no wish to fight with the Americans. "There is plenty of room for us both", they would say.

But that was not the attitude of the conquerors. The aboriginals were in their way. They wanted not just to enclose the common land, but also to take over those areas where minerals such as gold were to be found. On top of this, the civil war had just finished. There was a type of man about, who had developed a taste for fighting. This man had at his disposal a number of new and destructive weapons which had been invented during the war. Men like this made up most of the army which the United States' government used to put pressure on the redskins. This government was very distant from the Indians, did not understand them at all and was ready to listen to all the libellous and misleading stories invented by those who where anxious to make money out of the Indians' land.

On the whole, it would be true to say that the white men dealt completely dishonestly with the Indians. On almost every occasion, it was the soldiers who fired the first shot, even though the Indians sent envoys of peace under a white flag to try to make peace. All this shows that the Americans had every intention of driving the Indians from their native lands. Some of the white men's actions can only be explained by stating that they considered the Indians as less than human. Their sufferings were beyond description. When they saw there was nothing else they could do, they fought bravely, and at times successfully. But they had no real chance. Their weapons were bows and arrows and some old cannons, and their enemies were so numerous that they were almost always surrounded.

This book contains statements by several of the chiefs. What strikes the reader is their wisdom, their moderation, and the soundness of their reasoning. Much of what the other side said, on the other hand, is stupid, deceitful, and completely unreasonable. Agreements were made with the Indians and then broken as soon as the pioneers and their supporters pressed the government to do so. The story is sad in the extreme, and it makes the blood boil exactly as the blurb claims. I can only urge you to read the book. Here was yet another of the primitive peoples of the world who had followed a particular way of life since time immemorial; a way of life which was beautiful and in keeping with nature itself. It was confronted by the mechanised way of life, a money-gathering life based on the machine and the gun, and like every other culture, it collapsed before this soul-less Leviathan.

As I read this book, I could not help thinking of myself. Of course, one of the boasts of the English and their admirers is that they are less inhuman than other races. There is some truth in this assertion. What evil they do, they do wearing kid gloves, as it were. The sufferings of the Welsh are not to be compared with those of the Indians, although the decline of the Welsh has been going on for centuries. But there are comparisons to be made between them, and contrasts, each extremely significant. For instance, Wales was conquered by the English and our best land taken. Nowadays of course, it won't do to talk about violence. Our land today is being taken over by the English completely legally, according to English law, namely by means of money, and most of our fellow Welshmen do not care at all, so long as they make a profit. Again, the conquerors usually have things which appeal to those they conquer. The Indians were not hostile to the white man. Their aim was to live peacefully with him. Indeed there was considerable difference of opinions in their councils. Some held that the best thing was to do as

the white man wished. The future was his. Some went so far as to
serve as scouts to the soldiers, showing them the hiding-places of the
other Indians. You see the comparison. As long ago as Glendower,
there were Welshmen who believed that the future lay with the
English. That was why he failed. And the process continues. And
woe betide anyone who suggests using force to stop it. Our wish is to
live at peace with the English, to the point of servility. They too want
to live at peace with us—on their own terms.

But those Indian leaders who admired the white man were
exceptions. The chiefs said time and again that they did not like his
ways. One after another they pleaded with the President to pull back
the pioneers from the territories which they had entered illegally.
They wanted to live there themselves, following their ancient way of
life and worshipping the god of their fathers and grandfathers, the
Great Spirit; the only owner of the land.

When I was younger, I used to dream of a different society in
Wales. The population was comparatively small; there was a
distinctive language; there was space. Most of the country had not
yet been built on; most of the inhabitants worked on the
land—except for the industrial monster in the south. Language is
important; it partly reflects the personality of a people and it partly
moulds it. Would it not be possible, by means of Welsh, to avoid the
over industrialisation that had taken place in England, the
bottomless pit into which so many western countries were rushing?
The years went by. The industrialisation increased. The Welsh
countryside was covered with forests; the cottages and smallholdings
were taken by Englishmen. The dream receded. Today, having read
this book; having realised that the Indians, with their comparatively
simple ideas, were right; having begun to realise the extent of the
crisis which faces England and its imitators because of its over-
industrialisation, its over-population, the greed of its businessmen,
the wish to turn these islands into a shop in which others can buy, I
see that the dream was not so unfounded after all. The world is
round. This means that there are limits. Resources are limited; the
environment is fragile. They must be looked after and cared for as
the Indians knew instinctively.

The Welsh nation is not finished yet. The language is still alive.
We have not yet been put into a reservation to scrape a living there.
There are intelligent, sensible people among us. Our air and our
streams have not yet been polluted. Right is on our side. Rise up,

you Welsh, demand leaders of your own choosing to govern you in your own country, to help you to make a future in keeping with your own best traditions, before it is too late.

Note

1. A section of this review has already appeared in translation in *Planet*, 49/50 (1980), p. 111.

Bibliography

Bibliography of R.S.Thomas's Prose

(This list has been restricted to items that have appeared in a printed form. Transcripts of interviews are not included.)

1941 [Review of] '*The Good Pagan's Failure* by Rosalind Murray', *The Dublin Magazine*, XVI:3 (1941), pp. 67-68.

1944 [Letter to Keidrych Rhys], *Wales*, III:4 (1944), pp. 106-107.

1945 'The Depopulation of the Welsh Hill Country', *Wales*, V:7 (1945), pp. 75-80.

1946 'Arian a Swydd', *Y Fflam*, I:1 (1946), pp. 29-30.

'Replies to *Wales* Questionnaire 1946', *Wales*, VI:3 (1946), pp. 22-23.
'Some Contemporary Scottish Writing', ibid., pp. 98-103.

1947 [Review of] '*Break in Harvest and Other Poems* by Roland Mathias', *Wales*, VII:26 (1947), p. 323.
'Tenth Anniversary Year Message', ibid., p. 257.

1948 'A Welsh View of the Scottish Renaissance', *Wales*, VIII:30 (1948), pp. 600-604.
'Anglo-Welsh Literature', *The Welsh Nationalist*, (December 1948), p. 3.
'Dau Gapel', *Y Fflam*, 5 (1948), pp. 7-10.
[Translation of] ' "The Guests" by Dilys Cadwaladr', *Wales*, VIII:29 (1948), pp. 541-543.

1949 [Review of] '*The Gorse Glen* by E. Morgan Humphreys', *Y Fflam*, 8 (1949), pp. 55-56.

1951 [Review of]'*Welsh Odyssey* by R. G. Lloyd Thomas', *Y Fflam*, 10 (1951), pp. 53-54.

1952 'Llenyddiaeth Eingl-Gymreig', *Y Fflam*, 11 (1952), pp. 7-9.

[Review of] '*The Roses of Tretower* by Roland Mathias', *Dock Leaves*, III:8 (1952), pp. 34-35.

1956 'A Cymric Survey: [Review of] *A History of Welsh Literature* by Thomas Parry, trans. by H. Idris Bell', *The New Statesman*, 24 March 1956, p. 286.

1958 'The Welsh Parlour', *The Listener*, 16 January 1958, p. 119.

1959 'The Qualities of Christmas', *Wales*, 46 (1959), pp. 17-20.

1960 [Review of] *'Dragons and Daffodils: Contemporary Anglo-Welsh Verse* ed. John Stuart Williams and Richard Milner', *The Listener*, 8 September 1960, p. 393.

1961 [Editor of] *The Batsford Book of Country Verse* (Batsford: London, 1961).
Poetry Book Society Bulletin, 30 (1961), n.p.
'The Making of Poetry', *The Listener*, 17 August 1961, p. 250. [Text of broadcast 'The World of Books', producer A. P. Pearce, B.B.C. Home Service, 29 July 1961.]

1962 [Review of] *'The Oxford Book of Welsh Verse* by Thomas Parry', *The Listener*, 26 April 1962, pp. 740 & 743.

1963 [Editor of] *The Penguin Book of Religious Verse* (Penguin: Harmondsworth, 1963).
[Letter to the editor] *The Listener*, 14 November 1963, p. 797.

1964 [Editor of] *Selected Poems of Edward Thomas* (Faber & Faber: London, 1964).
Words and the Poet (UWP: Cardiff, 1964).

1966 'A Frame for Poetry', *TLS*, 3 March 1966, p. 169.

1967 'Adaryddiaeth—Beth amdani?', *Barn*, 52 (1967), pp. 94 & 96.
[Editor of] *A Choice of George Herbert's Verse* (Faber & Faber: London, 1967).
[Preface to] *MacDiarmid: The Scottish National Library Exhibition Catalogue* (Edinburgh, 1967), pp. 3-4.
[Review of] *'Barbarous Knowledge* by Daniel Hoffman; *W. B. Yeats and Georgian Ireland* by Donald T. Torchiana; *T. S. Eliot: Moments and Patterns* by Leonard Unger; *The Craft and Art of Dylan Thomas* by William T. Moynihan', *Critical Quarterly*, IX:4 (1967), pp. 380-383.

1968 [Answer to questionnaire] 'Poets on the Vietnam War', *The Review*, 18 (1968), pp. 43-44.
Poetry Book Society Bulletin, 59 (1968), n.p.
'St Davids', *By Request from Ten to Eight on Radio 4* (BBC: London, 1968), pp. 26-27 [Text of broadcast 'St David's' in the series 'Ten to Eight', producer Rev.J.Owen Jones, Radio 4, 1 March 1968.]
The Mountains (Chilmark Press: New York, 1968).

1969 'The Making of a Poem', *Conference of Library Authorities in Wales and Monmouth-shire 35th, Barry, 1968*, ed. L.M.Rees (Swansea, 1969), pp. 32-38.

1971 [Editor of] *A Choice of Wordsworth's Verse* (Faber & Faber: London, 1971).
[Letter to the editor, also signed by others] *The Times*, 28 May 1971, p. 17.

1972 *Y Llwybrau Gynt 2*, ed. A.Oldfield-Davies (Gwasg Gomer: Llandysul, 1972), pp. 7-25.
'Ynys Enlli', *Barn*, 121 (1972), pp. 16-17.

1974 [Review of] *'Bury My Heart at Wounded Knee* by Dee Brown', *Barn*, 135 (1974), pp. 102-103.
'Where do we go from here?', *The Listener*, 8 August 1974, pp. 177-178.

1976 *Abercuawg* (Gwasg Gomer: Llandysul, 1976).
[Letter to the editor, also signed by others] 'Cronfa Cartref John Jenkins', *Y Faner*, 16 January 1976, n.p.

1977 'Gwahaniaethu', *Y Faner*, 19 August 1977, p. 19.
'Hunanladdiad Y Llenor', *Taliesin*, 35 (1977), pp. 109-113 [Translated as 'The Creative Writer's Suicide', *Planet*, 41 (1978), pp. 30-33.]
'O'n cwmpas', *Y Faner*, 4 March 1977, p. 9.
[Letter to the editor] 'Yr "Union Jack" ', *Y Faner*, 20 May 1977, p. 16.
'Miwsig yn fy mywyd', *Welsh Music*, V:6 (1977), pp. 44-46.

1978 [Letter] 'Dwyieithedd?—Dim Perygl!', *Y Faner*, 25 August 1978, p. 6.
'The Creative Writer's Suicide', *Planet*, 41 (1978), pp. 30-33 [A translation of 'Hunanladdiad Y Llenor', *Taliesin*, 35 (1977), pp. 109-113.]
'Yr Ynys Dawel', *Y Faner*, 10 February 1978, pp. 5-6.

1979 [Letter] 'Achub y Gymraeg', *Y Faner*, 20 July 1979, p. 5.
[Letter] 'Nid yw Enlli yn eiddo'r genedl', *Y Faner*, 12 October 1979, p. 5.
[Letter supporting the principle of devolution, also signed by others] *The Western Mail*, 27 February 1979, p. 10.
[Letter] 'Trychineb', *Y Faner*, 27 July 1979, p. 4.

1980 'Llanw Llŷn', *Y Faner*, 7 November 1980, p. 10.
[Open letter addressed to William Whitelaw, also signed by others] 'Llythyr Agored', *Y Faner*, 20 June 1980, p. 4.
'Pe medrwn yr iaith', *Y Faner*, 11 January 1980, p. 4.

1981 [Letter] 'Atal y dreth incwm', *Y Faner*, 22 May 1981, p. 3.
[Letter] 'Difaterwch llethol', *Y Faner*, 17 July 1981, p. 4.

1982 'Neges R.S.Thomas', *Y Faner*, 30 April 1982, p. 1.

1983 [Letter] 'Cau ceg er mwyn chwe chant', *Y Faner*, 15 April 1983, p. 18.
'Araith R.S.Thomas', *Y Glorian Ddyddiol* ('Steddfod '83), 6 August 1983, p. 2.